THE Cruising Handbook

A step-by-step guide to booking wisely, planning ahead, spending less, and HAVING THE BEST CRUISE EVER!

KEVIN STREUFERT, MCC

kevin.streufert@cruiseplanners.com
888.958.1364

THE Cruising Handbook

ISBN-10: 1540352609
ISBN-13: 978-1540352606

Edited by Rita Grusing
Cover design by Kevin Streufert

Proper usage rights and permissions for photos and other images in this book were acquired through ShutterStock® and GraphicStock®. Additional photos were taken by the author himself.

This is a wholly original work derived from extensive research and the author's personal knowledge as a travel professional, world-traveler, and veteran cruise passenger. Any similarities to other published works is unintentional. However, common conclusions and recommendations with other travel experts relative to common travel situations should be expected.

TABLE OF CONTENTS

CHAPTER 1: GETTING STARTED

From the Author

There are plenty of cruising guides out there written by veteran travelers, each of whom shares valuable tips and tricks to enhance your voyage at sea. They're all great, so why listen to me?

Like the rest of my fellow authors, I am a veteran cruiser and world traveler. But I have a distinctive advantage: *insider knowledge*.

I am a travel professional who owns a Cruise Planners® travel agency and consults with clients every day, primarily about cruises. I hold a *Master Cruise Counsellor* (MCC) designation, granted by the Cruise Lines International Association (CLIA) after an extensive program of classroom and online training, exams, case studies, personal cruise experience, ship inspections, significant client bookings, and attendance at industry events. I am ever-immersed in continuing education and stay at the forefront of cruise industry developments every day.

I am also a published author with over a dozen books and numerous magazine and newspaper articles to my credit. That means I'll provide you with valuable information in a well-written and organized manner so you can easily consult the information of interest, put my recommendations into action, and move on with your busy life. The last thing I'll do is waste your valuable time.

You also won't catch me attempting to sway you toward my personal tastes regarding cruise lines, ships, or classes of service. Instead, I will lay out the facts and let you decide what's right for you. Everyone has different likes, dislikes, budgets and standards, so it is unlikely that your needs and preferences are the same as mine.

This book is primarily about ocean cruising, but you'll find an entire chapter dedicated to river cruising including summaries of the most notable river cruise lines and itineraries. River cruising is less complicated than ocean cruising, hence the single chapter on the subject. But if you're looking for a quiet, intimate vacation with cultural immersion, personalized service, a lack of crowds, and simplified embarkation/debarkation, it's a fantastic option.

This material is geared primarily toward North American citizens but should still be helpful to people in other parts of the world, especially to English-speaking travelers from the United Kingdom, European Union, Australia and elsewhere.

The cruise lines referenced herein are those accounting for 99% of worldwide bookings, but that doesn't mean there aren't some smaller companies out there worthy of your consideration.

My objective is to teach you how to handle an entire cruise vacation on your own, from the moment you begin your search to the day you return home from your trip. Nevertheless, I still recommend using an experienced travel agent/advisor when booking a cruise, and you'll read more about that in **Chapter 8**.

If you are in need of an agent, please feel free to shoot me an email or give me a call. You'll find my contact information below.

All my best, and bon voyage!

Kevin Streufert, MCC
kevin.streufert@cruiseplanners.com
888.958.1364

P.S. If you're a word geek like me, you might find the following two items interesting: First, you'll discover that I use the words "cabin" and "stateroom" interchangeably. They are one and the same. Second, you'll see the words "on board" and "onboard". "On board" is an idiomatic phrase, such as: "I could feel the party atmosphere when I stepped on board." The word "onboard" is an adjective, such as: "Kevin snagged a fantastic onboard credit for my cruise."

How to Use This Handbook

If you've cruised before, you already know how involved a cruise vacation can be, and there are so many secrets first-time cruisers wish they had known before booking their voyage, much less stepping on a cruise ship.

Even veteran cruisers learn a new trick each time around, and I hope to offer another tip or two to those readers, helping to take their experience to the next level.

Just about any cruise is a great cruise, but why not make it the best cruise it can be and save as much money as possible along the way?

Before we get into the meat of things, let's talk about the way this handbook is laid out and how to use it. If you only need advice on certain areas of your cruise vacation, feel free to save time by consulting the table of contents and jumping forward to your desired subject.

If you haven't booked yet, I encourage you to review the first several chapters, even if you're working with a travel agent, as they will provide valuable insights into your cruise selection process. Your agent will ask you plenty of questions to help find the right cruise for you, but every piece of additional information you provide to them will improve the ultimate results.

Chapters 2 through 6 are intended to familiarize you with cruising in general and help address the primary considerations before booking a cruise, listed here in sequential order:

1. Region – where do I want to go?
2. Cruise Lines – who do I want to take me there?
3. Ships – what kind of vessel do I want to sail on?
4. Departure Port – how far will I travel to meet my ship?
5. Target Travel Dates – when do I want to go?
6. Sailings/Itineraries – what's available?
7. Stateroom & Price – what's the best room I can afford?

We'll dig deeper into these seven subjects in **Chapter 7**, but I encourage you to keep the first five in mind as you read through the chapters in between. They represent the criteria for your cruise search, and I suggest making detailed notes on all five subjects as you go. You may not think I can help you with number 5, but some cruise regions have limited seasons, and you'll read about those in **Chapter 3**. That means I actually can!

The strategy here is to nail down your criteria so you aren't haphazardly sifting through hundreds or thousands of sailings, wondering which cruise lines or itineraries might be the best for you. *That* is a mind-numbing process, and I receive lots of calls from people who are ready to throw in the towel after such an exercise, begging me to put them out of their misery.

Instead, let's establish a list of criteria that whittle down your cruise selections to a digestible list and prepare you to make an informed, straightforward decision.

Once you've picked your ideal cruise, we'll move on to the best practices for booking it and how to save you the most money. Then, we'll personalize your trip to suit your own tastes, needs and requirements.

After that, you'll be all set, right?

Well, not exactly.

The remainder of the book, starting with **Chapter 9**, is where you'll find the most valuable information of all. It reveals how to plan ahead, avoid hiccups, and maximize every aspect of the cruise from your initial preparations at home through your entire vacation. This is where you'll learn how to cruise like a veteran, utilizing my insider tips as if you've already taken a dozen or more cruises, with all the valuable knowledge that came with them.

These insider tips appear throughout the book (in special boxes), and they'll pave the way for you to enjoy your voyage to its fullest while getting the most out of every dollar you spend.

Ideally, after reading this handbook, you'll eliminate any major surprises and never run across a situation on a cruise where you'll wonder, "what in the blazes should I do now?"

KEVIN STREUFERT

CHAPTER 2: INTRODUCTION TO CRUISING

Experiencing the Magic

Without a doubt, cruising the world's oceans and rivers is a unique type of vacation and arguably one of the best trips you will ever take.

You'll unpack just once to visit a multitude of exotic destinations and be transported from one to the next on the equivalent of a floating city. Add all the food, beverages and nonstop entertainment you could possibly hope for, and what's not to love?

Cruises have so much to offer, especially the opportunity to *explore*. It's quite different from spending an entire week at one destination to become immersed in the culture, which certainly has its own merits. But if those are the only vacations you take, you won't make it to some of the world's fascinating destinations. Life just isn't long enough, sobering as that may be.

Besides, it is both exciting and soul-enriching to wake up in a new port almost every day of your vacation with the prospect of exploring someplace new, and you'll return home to tell your friends and family, "guess what? We did this…and this…and this…and THIS!"

Just a quick look at the table of contents reveals how many cruise lines there are, and it's even more remarkable when you consider that this isn't a comprehensive list. The cruise lines covered in this book represent about 99% of the world market, but there are numerous smaller operators all over the world. That begs the question whether there's enough business out there to keep them all "afloat".

According to CLIA (Cruise Lines International Association, the world's oldest and largest cruise industry trade organization), 25.8 million passengers cruised in 2017, up from 24.7 million in 2016, and 2018 will easily surpass 26 million. Cruise ships consistently sail at or near capacity, despite the delivery of 13 new ocean cruise ships and 13 new river cruise vessels in 2017 alone. Last-minute specials, once considered a rule in the cruise industry, are now the exception, and they are typically limited to less-desirable sailings and/or older ships.

Cruise lines have similarities to each other, especially in their particular industry segment, but each has a unique culture and operating practices, even among those owned by the same parent company. For example, Carnival Corporation is the largest cruise line holding company in the world, but each of its brands are unique and operate autonomously.

Holland America and Princess are both Premium brands under Carnival's ownership, but passengers who have sailed on both lines can attest to the significant differences in their onboard experience.

Usually, veteran cruisers sample several brands until they find one that resonates with them—much like a make of car or hotel chain—and they tend to stick with it.

If you peruse through cruise line websites, you'll notice that all of them claim to offer the best food at sea, entertainment that is second to none, and an onboard culture that's ideal for all types of passengers, including families. In reality, no cruise line can be all things to all people, so allow me to objectively differentiate them for you, identify who has the best of what, and help you make a well-informed decision.

What Do Cruises Include?

One term you have probably heard people use when referring to cruises is "all-inclusive". However, with the exception of a few Luxury lines, cruises are in fact "mostly inclusive". That being said, a person can easily step on board any cruise ship without spending another dime on top of their cruise fare for the duration of the voyage and still have a great time, especially if they  don't drink alcohol. The only exception to this is your automatic daily gratuity charge, which we'll cover later.

All cruises include your stateroom, transportation on the ship from port to port, a large selection of food and restaurant choices, most onboard entertainment, and a varying degree of non-alcoholic beverages such as basic brewed coffee, filtered tap water, milk, and perhaps even juices or soft drinks at meals. Cruises also include your cabin steward, waiters and other service staff, although most of their income is covered by the above-referenced daily gratuity charge.

Except for a few companies in the Luxury segment, cruises usually *don't* include alcoholic beverages, gourmet coffees, specialty restaurants, organized shore excursions, child care, WiFi, or transportation to and from the ship. There are also plenty of discretionary items on which to spend money during a cruise from casino games and duty-free store purchases to spa treatments and professional photographs taken by the cruise line's onboard photographers throughout the voyage.

Some Luxury lines include everything in the "don't" list above, and they may even provide air travel to and from the ship. This includes international flights, sometimes even in business class for suite guests. If something is viewed as an amenity that most or all passengers would typically purchase, it is usually included in a Luxury cruise fare. Discretionary and personal items are always extra.

Above all, it is important to consider the value of everything included in your cruise fare or overall package in order to properly compare cruises and cruise lines to each other. For example, you may look at the fares for Silversea and immediately count them out. Yet, when you consider everything included in their fares and add all those items to a less-inclusive cruise, Silversea's pricing may not seem all that unreasonable.

Cruise Line Segments

Mass Market

Mass Market cruise companies, sometimes referred to as "Contemporary" or "Popular" lines, usually offer the most affordable fares in the industry, but that doesn't necessarily mean a higher-end cruise line is a better choice. It all depends on what you have in mind for your vacation.

For example, let's say you're an older couple with plenty of disposable income who would normally choose a luxurious sailing on Seabourn. However, you've decided to take your entire family on a cruise this time, including all the grandchildren, which makes Seabourn a less ideal choice, as it isn't geared toward kids. Instead, you might choose an Oasis-Class ship on Royal

Caribbean to ensure each generation has the onboard amenities they want. You can book a luxurious two-story suite with butler service for yourselves and put everyone else in standard staterooms. Then, to get the quality of food you've grown accustomed to, you can eat most of your meals in the specialty restaurants. This is one of the many ways to organize a group or family cruise to ensure that no one ends up disappointed.

There can be a significant price disparity within the Mass Market segment itself. Disney, for example, is a more expensive line that is often classified as Mass Market, but you'll see that I categorize it as a Niche line as well.

Mass Market ships are typically larger, family-friendly vessels with extensive recreational facilities that may include elaborate kid zones, multiple swimming pools, rock-climbing walls, multi-story slides, surfing simulators, ziplining, mini-golf, ice skating, carousels and even bumper cars. Passengers can also expect an extensive selection of dining options, bars, lounges and entertainment venues, giving them a wide range of choices for how and where to spend their evenings.

In other words, if you're looking for a true party atmosphere without any stuffiness, this is where you want to be.

Of course, larger ships mean a lot of passengers (typically in the 2,000 to 3,500 range, but possibly as high as 6,000), thereby resulting in a few trade-offs. The first is less personalized service than a Premium or Luxury brand, although

being waited on hand and foot isn't high on everyone's priority list.

Crowds are another potential concern, but they are usually limited to embarkation, debarkation and the occasional lines at dining venues. Otherwise, modern-day cruise ships are designed for optimal traffic flow and crowd reduction, giving passengers the feeling that the ship isn't very full, even if it's sold to capacity. Look for recommendations later in this book to avoid crowd-related issues even further.

Entertainment on Mass Market ships is often mainstream and sometimes over-the-top, with shows created by award-winning producers or choreographers, if not full-fledged Broadway musicals. You won't find performances like these on smaller luxury ships, even at those higher fares, because there just aren't enough revenue-generating passengers to justify the production costs.

Again, a higher-end cruise line doesn't necessarily mean you'll have a better experience, as it may not offer the amenities and entertainment you're looking for. It's important to determine in advance what you really want and choose the cruise experience with the best fit.

Mass Market cruise lines have made incredible improvements to their cuisine over the last decade or so, often hiring top chefs to create new dishes for their main dining rooms. Nevertheless, food in main dining rooms still suffer somewhat from the banquet-esque setting. It is impossible to crank out so many servings of food to a large crowd of people in such a massive venue and still give each plate special attention. That being said, one can still enjoy delicious main dining room meals throughout a cruise by being smart about their choices, such as leaning toward less complicated dishes and selections that are still tasty after losing their heat.

If you are a foodie, I highly suggest focusing on the specialty restaurants, where each meal is made from scratch with the finest ingredients. It's more comparable to a dining experience at the best restaurants on land. This is one of several upgrades one can add to a Mass Market cruise to achieve a Premium or Luxury experience at a lower overall cost—something I'll address in more detail later.

Mass Market is the only segment where you'll encounter true megaships like the aforementioned Oasis-Class vessels from Royal Caribbean, which weigh in at 225,000 gross tons and carry over 6,000 passengers at maximum capacity. To put this into perspective, an Oasis-Class ship has roughly the same displacement (actual mass) as a Nimitz-Class aircraft carrier. They are the closest thing in this world to a floating city, but only so many ports are capable of accommodating them, thereby limiting their menu of destinations.

Mass Market Summary: Lower fares, larger ships, high passenger count, family-friendly, extensive entertainment, many recreational options, numerous dining venues, best food in specialty restaurants.

Premium

Premium cruise lines have many similarities to Mass Market brands, but most ships fall into the midsize and large categories, with an onboard lifestyle that is typically more refined. The focus here is on quality versus quantity, with staterooms offering more amenities, tasteful décor throughout the ship, multiple gourmet restaurants, sophisticated bars, and a selection of culturally oriented shore excursions and onboard activities.

This doesn't mean partying is out of the question, but the choices will be less extensive. For example, you are far more likely to find a jazz quartet or classical string ensemble playing somewhere on a Premium cruise ship than you would on a Mass Market vessel. In other words, you'll encounter more entertainment and activities geared toward a well-educated adult consumer, such as enrichment lectures (often given by world-renowned experts), destination talks, gourmet cooking classes, wine tastings, private wine dinners, and quiet relaxation in adult-only retreats.

Premium lines often impose limits to the number of passengers under the age of 18 on each sailing, thereby preserving a quieter, adult-oriented atmosphere throughout the ship. This is further evidence that the cruise industry sees Mass Market ships as the ideal segment for families.

Premium brands primarily target baby-boomers and empty nesters with high disposable income and a focus on the finer things in life. However, affluent parents sailing with their children are also somewhat common, with the parents' desire for an upscale cruise experience trumping the kids' facilities on Mass Market ships. Most Premium cruise lines still offer kid zones and programs, but they tend to be less extensive and often focus on enrichment-oriented activities over outright entertainment. Younger children won't encounter their favorite cartoon character bopping along the deck in life-size form either.

The spa is usually a prime focus with Premium cruise ships, and there may even be spa-themed staterooms with unique spa privileges, a "clean cuisine" spa restaurant, or a focus on elaborate spa packages and unique body treatments. This ties with the more upscale clientele who are likely to have already incorporated spa, massage, fitness and other healthy activities into their daily lifestyle.

Cuisine in the main dining room on a Premium ship is usually a step above Mass Market vessels, but you will still find the highest quality fare in the specialty dining venues. If you are an aficionado of land-based prime steakhouses, for example, you should limit ordering red meat to the chop house specialty restaurant.

Premium ships are also more likely to offer a few higher-end shore excursion selections including personalized tours via private transportation.

Premium Summary: Midsize to large ships, upscale staterooms, better cuisine (though specialty restaurants are still king), sophisticated décor, refined entertainment, high-end shore excursion options, emphasis on the spa, adult-focused yet still family-friendly with enrichment activities.

Luxury

The focus of a luxury cruise is on extravagance, serenity, epicurean cuisine, fine wines, sophisticated entertainment aimed toward a small group of highly affluent passengers, and cultural immersion at each port of call. Flashy onboard entertainment and raucous partying are not part of the plan here.

Luxury cruise lines are naturally the most expensive of all, but many find the experience to be worth the increased cost. In fact, the disparity in price between Luxury and Premium cruises are not always as large as they may seem at first look. For example, Luxury lines are often all-inclusive and may even incorporate round-trip airfare, sometimes even in business class for suite guests. Once you add airfare, alcoholic beverages, shore excursions, Internet, specialty restaurants, gratuities and other items to a basic Premium cruise fare, the Luxury option may not be all that more, so it's important to do the math. The question is whether the Luxury line experience is what you're really looking for.

Smaller ships with exceptional service and lavish staterooms are distinctive of the Luxury segment, with many ships offering all-suite accommodations and verandas. Crew members typically learn who you are on Embarkation Day, call you by name throughout the voyage, and have your favorite drink waiting for you when you step on board or arrive for dinner. The experience is highly personalized and intimate, with your needs being met almost before you realized you had them.

Many Luxury line vessels are similar to mega-yachts and include unique features like the rear, fold-out marinas on Windstar and Seabourn, where passengers can directly access the ocean for a wide selection of watersports.

To the extent a luxury ship offers specialty restaurants, they are usually included in the cruise fare, and the objective is to offer variety, not a higher quality cuisine. Given the limited number of passengers and generous crew-to-passenger ratios on Luxury cruises, all dining venues on the ship are capable of dedicating personalized attention to every plate, and a commitment to the finest ingredients and expert culinary preparations should be expected. More often than not, the executive chefs obtain many of their ingredients at ports of call, carefully selecting them at markets and specialty purveyors. Passengers may have the option to accompany him or her in lieu of an excursion.

Typically, shore excursions are also included in the fare for Luxury cruises, and the options are likely to focus on cultural immersion as well as other upscale experiences such as winery tours/tastings, gastronomy, art, history, archeology and music. Most likely, there will be one or more exclusive events that no other cruise line offers, such as a private classical performance at Ephesus in the evening while the ancient historical site is closed to the public.

These smaller luxury ships are also known for visiting ports that Mass Market and Premium vessels are unable to navigate because of their size. This creates a far less regimented port experience, similar to traveling on a private yacht. Small Ships may also overnight at the more important ports-of-call, thereby enhancing the passengers' cultural immersion.

> **Luxury Summary:** Small intimate ships, low guest-to-staff ratios, exceptional personalized service, handcrafted epicurean food, luxurious staterooms, cultural immersion, upscale and exclusive shore excursions, primarily adult passengers.

Niche

Cruise lines that fall into the Niche category vary in some fashion from other cruise lines, usually because of unique itineraries, special activities and/or a targeted passenger demographic. Any or all of these characteristics will drive higher fares, but passengers with a desire for the unique offerings are usually willing to pay for the privilege.

Cruise expeditions are a prime example, such as those to Antarctica or the Arctic, since specialized ships and unique recreational equipment are key to the experience. These vessels are typically small and hold fewer passengers, thereby spreading the operating costs across fewer guests and raising prices.

Disney Cruises is considered a Niche line as well as Mass Market because it offers popular Disney-themed experiences for kids (of all ages) that are unique to the brand. Other Mass Market lines have responded by offering their own extensive youth programs and facilities, usually hitching themselves to other children's entertainment dynasties like Dr. Seuss on Carnival and DreamWorks on Royal Caribbean (*Shrek, Madagascar, Kung Fu Panda*). But Disney's brand power continues to generate the greatest demand and, consequently, higher cruise fares.

Niche Summary: Unique destinations, activities, or clientele. Specialized ships and/or equipment is possible. Higher cruise fares.

Cruise Ship Sizes

The cruise ship you select is almost as important as the cruise line itself. It all depends on what you're looking for. In other words, there's no such thing as the "best cruise ship in the world" since no single vessel offers every possible amenity or advantage.

For example, sailing on a small, luxury mega-yacht is likely to offer you the most exceptional service and epicurean cuisine on the ocean, but you won't see a full-fledged Broadway musical or ride a zip-line across the open rear deck of the ship.

Opinions vary regarding the exact passenger count for each size classification, and the gross tonnage of the ship plays a part in the equation as well. Still, here are some general guidelines:

Small Ships:	Under 1,000 Passengers
Midsize Ships:	1,000 to 2,000 Passengers
Large Ships:	2,000 to 3,000 Passengers
Megaships:	Over 3,000 Passengers

An example of a cruise ship that doesn't quite fit into its designated slot is **Celebrity Reflection**, a 3,046-passenger Solstice-Class vessel operated by Celebrity Cruises. The passenger count suggests it's a Megaship. But if you consider the modest gross tonnage of 126,000, its lack of over-the-top amusement park amenities that most people associate with Megaships, and a layout more typical of Mid-Size to Large vessels, most experts would consider it a Large Ship. Since Celebrity is a Premium cruise line that focuses more on tasteful luxury with food & wine rather than space-hogging, adrenaline-pumping venues like surf-simulators and rock-climbing walls, it makes sense that their use of space would be more efficient and allow them to snag a higher passenger count on a somewhat smaller vessel.

Here is a more detailed discussion of each cruise ship size classification including the pros and cons of each:

Small Ships

Most Small Ships are geared toward super-luxury, exclusivity and exceptional service. They may also offer an authentic sailing experience. Cruises on these vessels tend to bring the most expensive fares, with the smallest mega-yachts at the top end of the scale. That's because the relatively high operating costs must be recouped through a smaller group of passengers, and the finer things in life aren't cheap to deliver either.

The biggest advantage of Small Ships is their ability to visit exclusive and romantic little harbors where larger vessels can't go. Once docked, the small number of passengers means an absence of bottlenecks when boarding the ship or going ashore. The experience feels exclusive and intimate, much like traveling on a private yacht.

Staterooms on luxury vessels in this size category are the most well-appointed at sea, and suites are more common than not. Most include balconies, with traditional mega-yachts being an exception to the rule. After all, if you were traipsing about the Mediterranean with a billionaire on his sleek mega-yacht, you wouldn't have a balcony there either!

As noted in the Luxury segment discussion, the cuisine on Small Ships is usually the highest quality at sea. On the other hand, there won't be an extensive selection of specialty restaurant venues, if any at all. Instead, variety will be achieved through multiple menu selections and a unique *carte du jour* for each night of the cruise, often influenced by what the chef obtains on shore.

A handful of Small Ships offer a fold-out marina at the stern of the ship when it's anchored, thereby offering passengers direct water access for jet-skiing, wind-surfing, kayaking, swimming and a variety of other watersports. This just isn't feasible with larger ships.

Masted sailing vessels in this category range from serious clipper ships, on which guests can participate in rigging the sails, to ultra-luxury ships, where the sails simply add an extra dose of nostalgia and charm.

The more serious sailing ships are likely to have modest cabins and no elevators. People with mobility concerns should think twice before booking those cruises.

Other potential negatives for Small Ships include fewer entertainment options in the evening, a smaller choice of public spaces for socializing, little or no facilities for children, and a more intense reaction to rough seas. The latter is of particular importance for those with motion-sickness concerns.

Small Ship advantages include an intimate group of like-minded travelers, exceptional service, a highly-personalized experience, and a lack of families on board (if that's what you're looking for). Some lines even enforce a minimum age requirement for sailing.

Midsize Ships

Very few cruise lines are building Midsize Ships these days, so the majority are older vessels that may or may not have been extensively refurbished. In other words, the disparity in quality is larger here than in any other size category.

For older ships that haven't been upgraded with the latest and greatest amenities and décor, fares tend to be more affordable. Depending on the cruise line and sailing, that draws either an older clientele or exactly the opposite—younger people with limited discretionary income who bunk together in triples and quads for a big onboard party, usually on 3 to 4-day Caribbean and Mexico sailings.

The *Norwegian Sky* out of Miami is a great example of the latter scenario.

On the other end of the spectrum, consider the Midsize Ships operated by Crystal Cruises and Oceania. Some are older, some are newer, but they are all meticulously maintained and regularly refurbished to deliver up-to-date amenities and design schemes that reflect a high level of luxury. *Crystal Serenity* was built in 2003, making her an older ship by today's standards, yet she continues to be one of the most awarded ships at sea.

Think of it like a Ritz Carlton hotel that has been around a few years. No one would expect to walk into a guest room and see any significant wear and tear or a tired décor because Ritz Carlton regularly updates and refurbishes their rooms with an eye on every fine detail. The same is true for Crystal and Oceania's Midsize Ships. The only difference is that their hotels travel around the world.

One cruise line that has bucked the trend by building a number of beautiful Midsize Ships over the last several years is Holland America Line. Their cruise industry niche leans toward the elegant transatlantic ocean liners of the past, which were Midsize Ships by today's standards. However, with HAL's introduction of the 2,650-passenger, 99,500-ton *ms Koningsdam* in 2016, they firmly dipped their toes into the Large Ship category. But don't let their traditional design scheme fool you. The latest additions to HAL's fleet include all the same modern conveniences and technological advances as other modern-day cruise ships.

Midsize Ships reflect both advantages and disadvantages of Small Ships and Large Ships, which is why some people find them a good compromise. For example, Midsize Ships take rough seas better than Small Ships, yet not as well as their larger counterparts. Specialty dining and entertainment choices are more plentiful, but they'll be limited. Lines and crowds will be manageable, yet hardly comparable to the "private yacht" experience of a Small Ship.

Cabins on older Midsize Ships tend to be small, and balconies are in short supply, chiefly due to age instead of the ship size. Cruise lines didn't start building ships with a focus on balconies until the early to mid-2000s, which resulted in a boost to overall cruise sales. Standard balcony staterooms generate the highest demand of all cabin categories, and people are happy to pony up extra bucks to get them.

You will find more venues with things to do on Midsize Ships, such as casinos, libraries and cyber cafés, but not the vast recreational choices you see on Large Ships and Megaships.

Large Ships

When it comes to deciding on an ideal cruise ship size, many people choose Large Ships. They're massive enough to handle rough seas with impressive stability, but not so large that they're significantly limited in the number of ports they can access. Recreational and dining choices tend to be extensive, offering plenty of variety. You are likely to find venues designed specifically for kids, from splash parks and video arcades to play centers and daycare facilities. Consequently, Large Ships are usually a better choice for families than Small or Midsize vessels.

You'll find more entertainment on a Large Ship, and the production quality – particularly in the main theater – will be significantly better than what you'll find on a Midsize Ship. Casinos are large, with an extensive selection of table games and slot machines that usually include the most popular versions found in Vegas.

An extensive selection of bars, nightclubs and even a dedicated discotheque are common, thereby providing a wider range of choices in music and other performances like stand-up comedy, game shows, trivia contests and bingo tournaments.

Staterooms tend to be small and cookie-cutter in nature, but most have balconies. Fares are usually reasonable because the operating costs are spread across a large passenger base. Still, that high guest count can result in lines at the buffet restaurant and particularly in the cruise terminals during embarkation and debarkation.

Quality of service takes somewhat of a hit because of the higher guest-to-crewmember ratio, but that doesn't mean service staff aren't just as friendly as they are on other sizes of ships. Courtesy and graciousness are hallmarks of cruise ship personnel, so expect to thoroughly enjoy interacting with them. This extends from a butler on a luxury ship, always at your beck and call, to a waiter by the pool on a Megaship that you flag down for the tropical drink of the day.

Megaships

According to our trusty chart, Megaships are those with a passenger capacity of 3,000 or more. But with the introduction of Royal Caribbean's 225,000-ton Oasis-Class ships in 2009 (*Oasis of the Seas* shown here), the parameters have  become skewed. These massive vessels can carry over 6,000 passengers (though the double-occupancy rate is 5,400), suggesting that they deserve a category of their own.

Megaships are owned and operated primarily by Mass-Market cruise lines, though some Premium brands like Princess and Celebrity offer vessels that technically fall into the Megaship category.

Because of the sheer size, these ships carry more passengers, which some people consider to be a negative. But modern cruise ships are cleverly laid out to help manage traffic flow and make the ship seem half full, even when its sailing at capacity. The only time you'll grasp how many passengers you've traveled with is during embarkation and debarkation at the cruise port(s). You may look around at the throngs of people at the end of the cruise, grappling with all their luggage, and wonder where they all came from.

On the positive side, Megaships have more space for passenger amenities, from restaurants and bars/lounges to entertainment venues and recreational facilities. Think multi-story water slides, zip lines, mini-golf, rock-climbing walls, outdoor aqua-theaters, enormous casinos, and sometimes even a few unexpected choices like bumper cars, ice-skating, indoor skydiving, go-carts, laser tag, and an old-fashioned carousel. These ships represent the floating amalgamation of a huge Vegas hotel with a casino, amusement park, and a hip downtown district with restaurants, bars, lounges and performance venues. Seriously, how cool is that?

Evening entertainment choices on a Megaship are usually so extensive that it's hard to imagine anyone tossing up their hands in futility and heading back to their cabin because "there's nothing to do". To the contrary, many people find it difficult to choose from the array of options on the evening's program.

Like Large Ships, Megaships offer smaller cookie-cutter staterooms (most with balconies) and lower overall pricing due to the economies of scale. On the other end of the spectrum, you can find huge suites like the two-story Crown Loft Suites (shown here) offered on the aforementioned

Oasis-Class vessels from Royal Caribbean. All that space allows the cruise lines to include a greater variety of stateroom and service choices.

Finding your way around one of these vessels can be a challenge. That's why I suggest thoroughly "exploring" the ship via deck plans in advance. It may still take some to get the lay of the land after you board, but most of these vessels have touch-controlled screens near the elevator banks to help you find the onboard venue you're searching for.

Finally, if you're concerned about motion-sickness, Megaships move the least on rough seas. I specifically recommend them to first-time cruisers who aren't sure how they'll handle being on a cruise in the middle of the ocean. Start big, and work your way down. Even better, start with a serene Alaska cruise before you head out to the open seas, though you won't find any true Megaships up there.

CHAPTER 3: CRUISE REGIONS

Alaska

Cruises to Alaska take place primarily from May to September, and the magic is all about experiencing the state's expansive natural beauty and wildlife, in and out of the water. These cruises also traverse the beautiful Inner Passage and stop at the charming coastal towns along the way—primarily Ketchikan, Juneau, Skagway and Sitka, although Sitka has significantly reduced the number of cruises stopping there each year.

Breathtaking fjords and glaciers take center stage on the water, while land-based excursions and cruisetours lead passengers to towering mountains, deep gorges, pristine lakes and spectacular waterfalls. This is a great opportunity to explore Denali National Park, see Mount McKinley up close, or venture into Canada's rugged Yukon Territory.

When it comes to ocean wildlife, Humpbacks and Orcas (killer whales) garner the most excitement, with otters, Stellar sea lions and seals adding to the party. People lose count of how many bald eagles they see along the way, and it's not unusual to encounter grizzly bears, black bears, moose, caribou or black-tailed deer while touring on land. In addition to eagles, Alaska has numerous species of beautiful and unusual birds for your viewing pleasure.

Alaska cruises typically offer one of two types of itineraries – a round-trip voyage out of Seattle or Vancouver, or a one-way cruise going either northbound or southbound between Vancouver and Anchorage (via Seward or Whittier).

Round-trip cruises place an emphasis on Alaska's charming towns and often include a stop in beautiful Victoria, BC. They traverse the Inside Passage and usually visit at least one glacier plus a fjord or two. Some shore excursions, particularly out of Skagway, offer an opportunity to explore Alaska's pristine wilderness and Canada's Yukon territory, with a plethora of other nature-centric activities along the way.

People who choose a one-way itinerary usually add a land segment beforehand (southbound) or afterwards (northbound), allowing them to explore Denali National Park, Mount McKinley, and the towns of Anchorage and Fairbanks. Some cruise lines offer "cruisetours" with a combination of land and sea components, sometimes including a rail segment, thereby taking all the guesswork out of the equation. Other travelers prefer to rent a Jeep or SUV in Anchorage and set out on their own, self-directed Alaska wilderness adventure.

One-way cruises typically spend more time visiting the glaciers, often with an extended stop in Glacier Bay to watch the towering hunks of ice smash into the water below.

TIP: Bring mosquitio repellent (in addition to sunscreen) on all your outdoor activities in Alaska. It may seem like mosquitoes wouldn't thrive in all that cold... but they do. In fact, there's a running joke in Alaska that the mosquito is their state bird!

Asia

As much as Alaska offers otherworldly experiences with its natural wonders, Asia delivers them with unique cities and villages, ancient temples and artifacts, and enchanting people with amazing food and unfamiliar cultural traditions. For those who take cruises to explore the world, it's hard to imagine anything more satisfying than waking up each morning to another exotic Southeast Asian locale, promising new wonders to nourish the soul. On top of all that, you'll unpack just once and spend each night on board the ship in a comfy stateroom with all the Western conveniences you could hope for.

Asia cruises span from Saudi Arabia to Japan, so there's a huge selection of fascinating destinations to create an endless number of compelling itineraries. Experience the decadence of Dubai or Abu Dhabi. Stop in India and see the Taj Mahal, up close and personal. Relish in the mystique of Indonesia's romantic villages. Be dazzled by Singapore, Hong Kong or Bangkok. Experience the wonders of China, South Korea and Vietnam. Or, sample the energetic coastal cities of Japan, one-by-one.

It's not unusual for a longer Asia cruise to start in the Mediterranean before traversing the Suez Canal into the Red Sea. They may also launch from Australia or New Zealand and head northwest to Indonesia. In fact, "longer" is the operative word when it comes to Asia cruises because there's so much to see and do, and it takes both time and money to get there in the first place. In other words, it hardly seems worth the journey over to Asia for a quick, 7-day sailing.

The average passenger age on Asia cruises (for the North American market) is higher, as retirees and people who can take two or three weeks away from work will comprise most of the guests on board. Sailings take place between October and April, usually on ships that spend the rest of the year in Alaska or the Mediterranean.

> **TIP**: Public restroom facilities in many Asian destinations can be primitive, including squat-only toilets with no toilet paper. So, be sure to carry sanitary wipes and hand sanitizer on shore. For the cleanest and best-equipped facilities, stick to major hotels and tourist-friendly restaurants.

Australia and New Zealand

"The Land Down Under" offers a remarkable diversity in landscapes and climates, not to mention unique wildlife, making it unlike anywhere else in the world. Attempting to adequately explore Australia's geography and natural wonders is a daunting task, so a cruise that circumvents the continent is a great way to get a sample. If you like, experience a little bit of each area and decide where you'd like to base a land-based vacation on the next visit.

Most people think of the Great Barrier Reef or the Outback when Australia comes to mind, but cities like Melbourne and Sydney are thriving metropolises with highly developed cultural arts and world-renowned architecture like the Sydney Opera House (shown above) and Harbour Bridge.

Australia is a huge land mass, and there is so much in and around it that you'll find a plethora of cruise itinerary options. Some will concentrate solely on Australia, others just on New Zealand, and a few more will explore nary more than the Great Barrier Reef. It's also not unusual to see an itinerary that gives you a taste of the South Pacific, especially if it's a repositioning sailing.

For itineraries that feature New Zealand—arguably one of the most lush and beautiful places on the planet—they often include stops in Auckland, Wellington, Napier, Dunedin, and may even visit Fiordland National Park on the South Island. You should plan at least two weeks to cover both countries. Even so, you will most likely stick to just the south side of the Australian continent.

Australia/New Zealand cruises take place year-round, but October to April is the sweet spot with the most itinerary choices. However, December through February is summertime in that part of the world, and it can get very hot. Be sure to prepare accordingly.

Much like Asia cruises, the time and cost to travel to Australia or New Zealand from North America is too significant to justify a quickie cruise. This is another destination best saved for a period when one can set aside two weeks or more for vacation.

TIP: Of all the cruise destinations in the world, Australia probably deserves an additional land-based stay the most. It will alow you to explore areas of its interior that a day-long shore excursion just can't reach.

Bahamas

Many people think of the Bahamas as part of the Caribbean, but they are technically located in the Atlantic Ocean, not the Caribbean Sea. Also, "The Bahamas" can refer to either the

archipelagic state (i.e., the country) or the larger island chain it shares with Turks and Caicos.

Bahamas cruises tend to be 3 to 7-day tropical getaway itineraries out of Miami, Ft Lauderdale, Port Canaveral, and sometimes even New York City. They typically include a stop in Nassau (Paradise Island) as well as a beach and watersports day at the cruise line's private Bahamian island. Longer cruises may add Freeport (Grand Bahama) or a couple of northern Caribbean islands like Tortola (British Virgin Islands) or St Thomas (US Virgin Islands).

This is an ideal and often inexpensive option for a quick escape to recharge your batteries, have a party weekend with friends, or whisk the kids away for a fun-in-the-sun vacation that offers all the extra recreational opportunities of a cruise ship. In fact, many people take Bahamas cruises and never step off the ship at the ports of call. With pools, deck lounges, cocktail waiters and all the comforts you could hope for at your fingertips, it's easy to understand why. Besides, with so many passengers on shore during the day, the ship's pool deck is uncrowded, quiet and relaxing.

Bahamas cruises take place year-round, and some ships remain on permanent assignment there. But, like Caribbean cruises, more sailings are available during winter months when demand is higher from those who crave getting away from the cold.

Ships that spend their summer months in Alaska and Europe may relocate to the Bahamas and Caribbean to add more choices and itineraries.

> **TIP**: If you've been thinking about a trip to Atlantis, consider a Bahamas cruise instead and opt for an Atlantis one-day-pass shore excursion (including the waterpark) while in Nassau. You'll probably spend less money and may just have more fun.

Baltic Sea

When you consider the diverse nations, contrasting languages and cultures, ancient histories, stunning architecture, artistic masterpieces, and breathtaking scenery that grace the Baltic Sea, it's easy to understand why cruises in this region are so enriching. In fact, there is no better way—financially or logistically—to experience all these amazing places than on a cruise.

Even better, it's only necessary to unpack once, with the end of each day placing you back on board a floating city with an English-speaking crew. You'll sleep each night in a comfortable bed, eat whatever food strikes your fancy, and have everything you could possibly want at your fingertips. Ah, the luxury of it all!

Baltic cruises originate from various ports, though most major cruise lines start from Copenhagen, Denmark or Warnemünde, Germany, with the latter offering easy connections to and from Berlin. Ships usually stop in Oslo, Stockholm, Helsinki, and Tallin (Estonia), but the *pièce de résistance* of a Baltic cruise is the magnificent city of St. Petersburg, Russia.

Most cruise ships spend the night in St. Petersburg, giving passengers two full days to explore the city's riches. Longer cruises might even give you a full or partial third day.

The best part about visiting St. Petersburg on a cruise is not having to deal with the complicated tourist visa requirements for visits via air or land. In essence, the licensed guide on your organized tour is your living, breathing visa, with the Russian government requiring him or her to supervise and keep track of you throughout the excursion. The idea is to ensure you stay with the group and return to your ship at the end of each day.

Other fascinating destinations a Baltic cruise might offer, especially if it's a longer voyage or a smaller ship, are Skagen (Denmark), Gdansk (Poland), Klaipėda (Lithuania), and a few other small destinations. They might even throw in a Western European destination like Amsterdam, Kiel, Zeebrugge (Bruges and Brussels), Le Havre (Paris), or Southampton (London), especially if the itinerary begins and/or ends in one of these ports.

Baltic cruises typically run from May to September, with the sweet spot being June to August because of the warmer temperatures. If you don't mind a little chilly weather, take advantage of the lower fares in May and September.

While arguably part of the Baltic, cruises that specifically concentrate on the Norwegian Fjords are discussed separately.

> **TIP**: It's easy to load up on shore excursions in the Baltic, and they are mandatory in St Petersburg. But, consider spending a relaxing day on your own in one or more of the other ports. A great place to do this is Tallin, Estonia where people are friendly, and flowers are everywhere. It feels like a charming Germanic village trapped in time.

Bermuda

Bermuda is a popular summer destination for cruisers and land vacationers alike because of its warm air and water temperatures, both

of which rise above the 80-degree mark from June through September.

This British Overseas Territory is situated in the Atlantic Ocean, approximately 665 miles east-southeast of Cape Hatteras, North Carolina. It's a tourist-friendly destination with beautiful pink-sand beaches, charming port towns, and several prime golf courses.

Most Bermuda-only cruises last 5 to 7 days, take place from April to early November, and originate from New York/New Jersey, Boston or Baltimore. Once there, cruise ships typically camp out for a few days at King's Wharf, allowing passengers to leisurely come and go as they spend time on the beaches, enjoy a variety of watersports, tool around the islands on a scooter, visit the museums, shop 'til they drop, or play a few rounds of golf. On occasion, ships may add a night or two in Hamilton or St George's.

Bermuda is also a popular cruise itinerary for honeymooners because of the extended, relaxing days at sea and an easy itinerary that doesn't entail multiple ports of call with countless, tempting shore excursions. In other words, if you're looking for a truly relaxing vacation with all the advantages of a cruise, this is a great way to save you from yourself.

Most Bermuda cruises take place during hurricane season in the Atlantic, which is officially June through November. In the event your cruise is disrupted by a storm, it may transform into a Canada/New England sailing (see next section), and the cruise line isn't obligated to compensate you for any inconvenience or disappointment that may result. The terms and conditions of passage for all cruise lines includes their right to alter itineraries at their discretion in order to preserve the safety of the passengers, the crew, and the vessel itself.

TIP: Bermuda can be expensive, so consider setting a daily schedule where major meals are enjoyed on board the ship, and set your expectations for the prices of any onshore purchases.

Canada & New England

Most people think of Canada & New England cruises as only for viewing fall foliage in late September and October, but there's so much more to see and experience in this amazing region of North America. The cruise season itself lasts from May through October, in part because spring and summer landscapes offer plenty of breathtaking colors as well.

What else is there to see? How about exploring the stunning Atlantic coast with its charming towns, historic sites, rugged cliffs, nostalgic lighthouses, dense forests and national parks? As you head northward, you can take in Canada's fascinating maritime provinces, including Nova Scotia, New Brunswick and Newfoundland. The area seems like a world of its own.

Eat the best mussels in the world, freshly harvested at Prince Edward Island—the gold standard for these tasty shellfish. Then, cruise down the St Lawrence River to Quebec City and Montreal for a little slice of France without the pricey transatlantic flights.

Outdoor activities also abound here, including whale-watching boat trips, kayaking, canoeing, hiking, biking and whitewater rafting. You can hop on a masted sailing vessel for an enjoyable ride or take a relaxing winery tour in seemingly unlikely places like Nova Scotia, Quebec and Maine.

There are essentially two types of Canada & New England cruise itineraries. The first is a round-trip voyage, usually out of Boston, New York City, Cape Liberty or Baltimore, which can be 7 to 10 days in length and will concentrate on the Atlantic coast. The second is a one-way itinerary, usually between Quebec City or Montreal and Boston or New York City, adding a cruise along the St Lawrence River, often with a stop at Prince Edward Island. Small-ship cruises may add Martha's Vineyard, Nantucket or other boutique ports that full-sized vessels can't access.

> **TIP**: Make sure to layer your clothing as you head out on excursions. Temperature variations between morning or evening and the middle of the day can be significant.

Caribbean

To the casual observer, the Caribbean may seem like a place to camp out on the beach, read a novel, enjoy the sounds of the surf, and catch some rays. While that sounds very relaxing, to be sure, the region offers so much more, making it the number one cruise destination in the world.

The most significant factor contributing to the Caribbean's appeal is the variation in cultures, from small freestanding nations to the many islands tied to countries around the world like Great Britain, France, The Netherlands, and the United States. The charm of all these colonial influences, especially in the Southern Caribbean, range from language and customs to architecture and cuisine, delightfully colored by local island influences.

The geographic characteristics of the islands throughout the Caribbean also vary significantly, from lush rainforests and mountains to desert climates and huge coral reefs. So, it's no wonder why an island-hopping cruise through this region is a feast for the soul as well as the senses.

Caribbean cruises are split into three regions—Western, Eastern and Southern—each with its own unique characteristics, as discussed in the subsections that follow. Cuba is also part of the Caribbean, but deserves its own itinerary topic because of the unique aspects of traveling there (for US citizens).

Caribbean cruises happen year-round, but peak season, with the largest selection of ships and itineraries, occurs from December through April. During this time, the Caribbean snaps up ships that sail Alaska, the Mediterranean, the Baltic and Western Europe during the remainder of the year.

Hurricane season lasts from June through November, but that doesn't stop cruises during this timeframe from selling out. Besides, several of the Southern Caribbean islands like Aruba, Curaçao, and Bonaire lie beneath the hurricane belt and are only impacted by hurricanes every 28.8 years.

Western Caribbean

Western Caribbean cruises are downright convenient. You can't beat the close proximity or selection of US departure ports including Miami, Ft Lauderdale, Port Canaveral, Tampa, New Orleans and Galveston. These factors make 3 and 4-day cruises feasible for those looking for a quick escape, including first-time cruisers who are eager to dip their toe into the water, so to speak.

Destinations span from the Yucatán Peninsula to Jamaica and may include Cozumel, Progreso, Costa Maya, Belize, Honduras, Grand Cayman and Jamaica itself. Key West and Nassau are popular additions for cruises sailing out of Miami and Ft Lauderdale, even though they are technically not part of the Western Caribbean.

This sub-region is ideal for watersports activities such as scuba diving and snorkeling (considered by many to be the best in the world), jet-skiing, parasailing, and deep-sea fishing. On land, one can visit numerous fascinating Mayan ruins, take a high-octane jungle Jeep adventure, go ziplining, or just relax on a pristine beach while drinking cocktails and listening to the waves.

TIP: Weather in the Western Caribbean can vary from intense sun to tropical rains, so be sure to carry everything from serious sun protection to a light waterproof jacket.

Eastern Caribbean

The choices of Mainland US departure ports may not be as plentiful as Western Caribbean cruises, but the selection of Eastern Caribbean *itineraries* is broader. This is due, in part, to the common addition of ports that are technically not part of the Eastern Caribbean at all, such as Nassau (Bahamas) and Turks & Caicos (West Indies). Cruise line private islands, most of which are located in the Bahamas, may also be added. But these cruises will still be billed as Eastern Caribbean if one or more qualifying ports of call are on the itinerary, meaning the British Virgin Islands, the US Virgin Islands, St. Maarten, or Puerto Rico.

Most Eastern Caribbean cruises originate from Miami, Ft Lauderdale, Port Canaveral and Jacksonville, but East Coast ports even farther north have entered the game, including New York, Baltimore, and Charleston. The East Coast's proximity to this island region allows for cruises of various lengths, usually ranging from 3 to 10 days.

Even though most people feel the Western Caribbean rules when it comes to beaches and watersports, the Eastern Caribbean is no slouch in that department. Yet, the distinctiveness here is the rich history and cultural influences of countries around the world, particularly from Europe. It's easy to pick out French, Dutch and British colonial attributes to this day.

This is also the best area in the Caribbean for shopping, with notable deals on jewelry in St Thomas (USVI). It helps that US Citizens are allowed to bring $1,400 worth of merchandise back from the US Virgin Islands without taxation. The island of Sint Maarten/Saint Martin gives all the others a run for their money with shops galore, especially on the Dutch side. Since the island is duty free, the bargains are that much better.

> **TIP**: Eastern Caribbean ports are often busy and crowded, but it's not difficult to find a serene spot on a beach or outdoor café a short distance away. Be sure to research your ports of call and set a beach strategy in advance.

Southern Caribbean

Because of its distance, international cultures and reduced influence from the United States, the Southern Caribbean is less traveled and more exotic than the other two Caribbean regions. It also contains more islands, though many of them are smaller and underdeveloped.

To get a sense of the rich cultural diversity here, just take an inventory of the islands and their colonial heritage. Aruba, Curaçao and Bonaire hail from the Netherlands. Martinique, St Barth's and Guadeloupe are French. Antigua, Dominica and Barbuda are under Great Britain's domain. Trinidad and Tobago form their own dual-island nation, but began as a Spanish colony with heavy influences from South America—particularly nearby Venezuela. Grenada was a French colony, then became a British territory, and finally became independent in 1974.

The Southern Caribbean's lack of proximity causes most cruisers to explore the Western and Eastern regions first. Once they've exhausted all those major destinations, their attention naturally turns to the alluring islands of the South. The problem is not being able to take a quick cruise out of Miami or Ft Lauderdale anymore.

Southern Caribbean cruises leaving from ports in the Continental US usually last 10 days or longer because of the added sea days it takes to get there. Alternatively, one can knock the cruise length down to a week by departing from San Juan, St Martin/St Maarten or Barbados. It is also common for Southern Caribbean ports of call to be included in Panama Canal or extensive South American cruises that depart from the continental United States.

TIP: If scuba-diving or snorkeling is high on your list, note that Curaçao and Bonaire offer some prime coastal areas for these activities.

Cuba

While Cuba is technically part of the Caribbean, the unique itineraries and travel restrictions for US citizens warrant a dedicated discussion.

Cruises to Cuba (for US citizens) are a relatively recent phenomenon, having sprouted up after the relaxation of travel limitations by the US Government in early 2015. Most significantly, it is no longer necessary for American citizens to obtain a special license to legally visit our communist island neighbor.

Regardless, as of early 2018, it is still ***illegal*** for US citizens to travel to Cuba for tourism. Your visit must fall into one of twelve special-purpose categories such as journalism, visiting family, participating in religious or cultural programs, or conducting humanitarian missions.

Most Americans travel to Cuba under "people-to-people" programs, which is a broad category that paves the way for a multitude of qualifying activities, and the shore excursions offered by cruise lines are specifically designed to comply.

US Passengers are also allowed to follow their own, self-directed onshore activities provided they keep detailed records, though word on the street is that no one ever checks.

In addition to complying with one of the 12 special-purpose categories, travelers to Cuba must buy a Visa (aka "Tourist Card"), but the cruise lines will obtain that on your behalf for around $75.

There are two primary itinerary choices for US citizens cruising to Cuba. The first, offered by several major cruise lines, is a simple stop in Havana for a day or two, during which shore excursions are offered in compliance with the above-referenced, people-to-people travel guidelines. The itinerary often combines this with other Caribbean or Bahamas destinations such as Key West, Cozumel, Jamaica and the cruise line's private island.

The second choice is a Cuba-only voyage around the island with stops in Havana, Cienfuegos, Santiago de Cuba and perhaps a few smaller ports.

During port days, US passengers spend time on shore engaging in humanitarian, educational or community development programs. On sea days and evenings, they enjoy a relaxing and comfortable cruise experience with a special focus on Cuban cuisine and cultural enrichment lectures or activities.

> **TIP**: US citizens are now legally able to bring $100 worth of Cuban cigars and/or rum back to the USA. Don't miss out!

Hawaii

Most people don't immediately think of Hawaii as a cruise destination, but there are some compelling reasons to see the 50th US state that way. Sure, you can check into a resort and relax on the beach for the duration of your stay, but if that's the only thing on the agenda, perhaps an all-inclusive resort in the Caribbean makes more sense. It will cost less, and you won't burn as much time in the air.

To truly experience the abundance of Hawaii, you need to hop from one island to the next. Each is surprisingly different, with its own unique treasures worthy of exploration on their own. You could accomplish this by spending half your time flying from one island to another, usually connecting each time through Honolulu, checking in and out of hotels while constantly packing and repacking your suitcase along the way. Alternatively, you could take a relaxing, 7-day voyage on Norwegian Cruise Line's *Pride of America*, unpack just once, and let your resort hotel follow you around the islands.

Repositioning voyages and world cruises that traverse the Pacific also frequently stop in Hawaii, and some lines offer seasonal round-trip Hawaii cruises out of San Diego, Los Angeles, San Francisco or Vancouver. For those departing from one of the aforementioned US ports, expect at least one stop in a foreign territory—usually Canada or Mexico—because of an outdated maritime law from the 1830s that prohibits foreign-registered passenger vessels (i.e., almost all cruise ships) from following a US-only itinerary.

So, how does Norwegian Cruise Lines operate a cruise ship strictly in Hawaii? They registered the *Pride of America* in the United States, of course, but there were three other restrictions to comply with as well. The vessel had to be built in a US shipyard, which *Pride of America* was, at least for the most part. The crew must be comprised entirely of US citizens paid under US minimum wage laws, which they are. And finally, the vessel's ownership must be a US company, hence why the ship is owned through a separate entity called NCL America.

Hawaii is also an ideal place to arrange for a rental car at one or more ports and head out to explore the island on your own rather than take an organized tour. This is the United States, after all, so it's just like renting a car in any other location throughout the mainland, with all the same rental agencies. You'll even find a similar selection of cars except for a preponderance of Jeeps and convertibles.

Like Caribbean cruises, you always have the option of spending your day at a beach, some of which will be in walking distance from the port.

> **TIP**: When it comes to Hawaiian coffee, people usually think of Kona from the Big Island. But, be sure to try the smooth yet equally robust coffee grown on Kauai. There's a visitor's center where you can sample every roast and blend.

Mediterranean

If I had to pick the top destination where my clients come back from a cruise and rave about having the trip of their lives, the Mediterranean would win hands-down.

First, there's the whole "fun in the sun" aspect, featuring some of the most beautiful beaches and unreal turquoise waters in the world. And, when you consider the smorgasbord of countries, cultures, sights, and marvels of ancient world history, no other cruise destination can compare.

The primary ports where Mediterranean cruises originate and terminate are Barcelona, Rome, Venice, Athens and Istanbul, all of which are worthy of thorough exploration on their own. But the myriad of destinations in between is so vast that it's hard to imagine scratching the surface in just a week or two. That's why the Mediterranean is a cruise destination that can be revisited again and again without exhausting all the possibilities.

The Greek Isles alone can monopolize a single visit, with the archeological wonders of Santorini, the infectious energy of Mykonos, and the picturesque beaches of Crete, among many others. There are plenty of islands worthy of exploration tied to other European countries such as Sicily (Italy), Sardinia (Italy), Corsica (France), and Mallorca (Spain). And how about the fascinating island nations of Cyprus and Malta?

When it comes to continental ports of call, Kuşadasi in Turkey offers passage to the ancient civilization of Ephesus. Dubrovnik and Split open the door to Croatia's treasures, including the lovely Dalmatian coast. And Kotor is the gateway to Montenegro's ancient charm, not to mention its wines, which are arguably the finest in the Balkans.

Farther to the west, we find Italian ports like Livorno, which offers convenient day tours to Florence and Cinque Terre. From Sorrento, we can visit the Amalfi Coast, Positano, Ravello, Naples, the island of Capri, and the ever-imposing Mount Vesuvius. French coastal towns like Nice, Toulon and Marseille let us experience the chic Côte d'Azur and the charm of Provence. Then, moving on to Barcelona, Valencia and Málaga, we experience the magical coast of Spain.

We haven't even talked about exploring the mysterious lands surrounding the Black Sea or visiting Cairo and the Great Pyramids. The possibilities are endless.

Mediterranean cruises generally happen from spring to fall, but you'll find the most sailings during summer months when they're in the highest demand. Winter cruises are also possible, offered primarily by European lines such as Costa, MSC and AIDA.

The Mediterranean is also an ideal destination for yachting or yacht-style experiences from cruise lines like Seabourn, Windstar, SeaDream Yacht Club, and Star Clippers.

> **TIP**: If possible, book your Mediterranean cruise for the late spring or early fall to get the best cruise fares. You'll also avoid the crowds and sweltering heat of summer.

Mexican Riviera

Cruises to the Mexican Riviera aren't as plentiful as they once were, with the blame pointed at a rash of violence in Acapulco and Mazatlán in 2011 that caused cruise lines to cut itineraries. It's a shame because this long stretch of beautiful Pacific coastline offers countless pristine beaches, prime deep-sea fishing, ideal conditions for water sports, fascinating ancient ruins, and a collection of tourist-friendly seaside towns with notable restaurants, bars, shopping, and in some cases a chic nightlife.

The Mexican Riviera stretches down the Baja Peninsula from Ensenada to Cabo San Lucas, then continues along Mexico's Pacific Coast from Mazatlán to Puerto Vallarta and Acapulco before hitting a number of smaller towns along the coastline toward the border with Guatemala. Some cruises even venture up into the Gulf of California (aka the Sea of Cortez) to visit charming towns like La Paz, Guaymas, Loreto and Topolobampo.

Sailings to this region take place year-round, although they are seasonal for most lines. Ships typically leave from Los Angeles and San Diego, but may start as far north as San Francisco. Mexican Riviera ports of call are also popular stops along the way for Panama Canal and Central American itineraries.

TIP: Mexico has made great strides since 2011 to reduce violent crime, especially toward tourists, but it's still advisable to stick to primary tourist areas or your organized tour. Also, leave your jewelry and other valuable items in your stateroom's safe while enjoying time on shore.

Norwegian Fjords

Cruises to the Norwegian Fjords usually begin in the Baltic Sea from ports like Oslo or Copenhagen. Their aim is different than a typical Baltic cruise, hence why I've listed them in a separate category. Instead of sailing to rich capital cities, Norwegian Fjords cruises concentrate on the beauty of nature and visiting sleepy little port towns that don't overwhelm visitors with numerous cultural and historical attractions.

In other words, a Baltic cruise is more of a go-go-go vacation, whereas a Norwegian Fjords cruise is more about relaxation.

A cruise may be the best way to see many areas of the world, but when it comes to the Norwegian Fjords, it's pretty much the *only* way. Sure, you could spend exorbitant

amounts of money on Norway's pricey land-based hotels, restaurants and ground transportation, hopping from one town to the next while hiring smaller boats to explore all the wonders of nature, but why? With a cruise, you'll unpack just once, enjoy easy transportation from place to place, and the majority of your food will be included. Besides, isn't it easier to let someone else handle all those pesky details and free you up to relax and enjoy the beauty?

Many of the beautiful fjords like Geirangerfjord, Aurlandsfjord and Sognefjord are easily navigable by your cruise ship, thereby reducing the number of separate tours to buy. Still, you'll probably opt for two or three to see sights you can't reach any other way.

Given the far northern geography involved, near or within the Arctic circle, Norwegian Fjord cruises run primarily from May to September, with the prime months being June, July and August.

> **TIP**: Despite the ease and savings of dining on board your ship, don't miss the unique foods you can at least sample on shore in Norway. This includes various types of salt-cured fish, reindeer, whale, elk, unique cheeses, and even a shot of a local aquavit (a flavor-infused distilled spirit).

Pacific Coastal

Pacific Coastal cruises generally focus on the North American West Coast from San Diego to Vancouver. A stop in Mexico, such as Ensenada, might be thrown in to comply with a law from the 1830s (see Hawaii) prohibiting any foreign-flagged ship from sailing on a US-only itinerary. The same thing can be achieved with a stop in Victoria or Vancouver, where many Pacific Coastal cruises begin or end.

In addition to the cities noted above, ports of call might include Nanaimo (British Columbia), Seattle, Astoria, San Francisco, Monterey, Santa Barbara, Los Angeles, and Catalina Island. Some itineraries are as short as two to five days, making them ideal and quick getaways for people in North America.

Pacific Coastal sailings occur year-round, but they aren't all that plentiful, and they may be tied to a ship's global repositioning to Alaska or elsewhere. Princess is the only year-round operator, with Holland America coming in second, offering sporadic Pacific Coastal cruises from spring to fall.

> **TIP**: It's not unusual to find 1 to 3-night sailings from various West Coast cities to Vancouver (or vice-versa) with inside cabin fares priced less than flying. Go from Point-A to Point-B and get all the gourmet food, entertainment, seafaring bliss and comfortable accommodations for free.

Panama Canal

For many people, traversing the Panama Canal on a cruise ship is a bucket list item. That's due in part to the remarkable history involved with the 100-year-old engineering wonder, but also because it's hard for full-time workers to carve out enough vacation time for the lengthy itineraries. That pushes the trip toward retirement for a lot of people, but with the advent of telecommuting and a handful of shorter itinerary choices, these sailings aren't as dominated by seniors as they used to be.

Panama Canal cruises initially consisted of itineraries in the 14-day range to and from Florida and the West Coast, with stops along the way in the Caribbean, Central America and Mexico. However, cruise lines have mixed things up over the last few years, offering sailings as short as 7 days and as lengthy as 21, with the longer trips typically comprised of repositioning sailings between Alaska and the Caribbean.

Shorter Panama Canal sailings are usually partial crossings out of Florida, whereby the ship stops roughly halfway in Gamboa, allowing passengers to experience a variety of shore excursions. One typical excursion option is passage through the rest of the canal on a smaller vessel in order to see the Gaillard Cut, Centennial Bridge and Bridge of the Americas. After everyone is back on board, the cruise ship reverses course and heads back toward Florida, potentially stopping in Colon (Panama), Cartagena (Colombia), or any of the Caribbean islands.

"The dream" for most people is to sail through the entire canal, spending a full day experiencing the locks and bridges along the way. They may even have the benefit of an expert lecturer, telling tales of the canal's illustrious history.

Panama Canal cruises run from October to April, but it's best to wait until December or later, after the rainy season in Central America has ended.

> **TIP**: On the day you navigate the canal, get up early to snag a space at the bow of the ship or in the observation lounge, even if you're staying in a balcony stateroom. You'll want a 360-degree view of "the process".

Polar Expeditions

Sailing to Antarctica or exploring inside the Arctic Circle isn't your everyday cruise, hence I refer to these voyages as "polar expeditions", even though passengers won't be venturing all the way to the South Pole. You'll find many specialty and expedition-type vessels navigating these waters, especially those venturing farther in, so this is not like hopping on a party ship in Miami and tooling around the Bahamas.

These cruises are otherworldly adventures with wildlife and natural wonders that very few have seen up close and personal. Think of the various species of penguins and seals hanging around

Antarctica or polar bears hunting from the ice in the Arctic. We're talking once-in-a-lifetime experiences here.

Antarctica sailings take place from November to March amidst the Southern Hemisphere's summer season, with December and January being the most popular. Days are longer, the weather is less severe, whales are frolicking in the water, penguin chicks are hatching, and the ice recedes to facilitate venturing farther south.

You have two possible cruise experiences in Antarctica. The first is on a mainstream cruise ship sailing around the safer waters, with views of the remarkable ice formations and plenty of marine life. Unfortunately, the International Association of Antarctica Tour Operators (IAATO) prohibit ships with more than 500 passengers from letting guests go ashore, so you won't have that opportunity. These larger ship visits are sometimes appended to a "round-the-horn" South America cruise.

The other option is to take a much smaller expedition ship with companies like Lindblad (Nat Geo), Hapag-Lloyd and a handful of others. These lines typically outfit their guests in parkas and cold-weather gear, then shuttle them to land on Zodiac boats to explore and encounter wildlife (particularly penguins) up close. It's also possible to swing a more luxurious Antarctica experience on the smaller cruise ships from Silversea, Seabourn and PONANT.

Arctic cruises are entirely the domain of expedition companies, such as those listed above, though a Norwegian Fjord cruise on a major cruise line might skate along the perimeter (i.e., the Arctic Circle). This is the polar bear capital of the planet—not to take anything away from walrus, seals, musk oxen, reindeer and arctic foxes—and expedition ship crews are experts at finding these amazing creatures for your viewing pleasure.

Of course, the season for Arctic cruises is the exact opposite of the Antarctic, lasting from May to September, with the sweet spot being July and August. At this midpoint of summer, the ice has retreated enough to allow ships to navigate farther north, in some cases even to the North Pole or through the Northwest Passage. Still, the window is short.

A handful of Arctic cruises are also available in winter months, primarily to see the Northern Lights (Aurora Borealis), which is rarely visible in the summer because of the nonstop daylight. These voyages also give guests the opportunity to participate in more intense winter activities.

> **TIP**: Expedition cruise lines and their organized excursions assume that guests are physically fit and capable of participating. If you aren't sure of your abilities or suffer from back, neck or other conditions that might be exacerbated by strenuous activity or forceful motion (such as in a Zodiac boat), consider a mainstream cruise line instead.

South America

Let's face it. South America is a massive continent, so you'll only cover a fraction of it on any given cruise. Even the popular round-the-horn itineraries, which usually last 14 days or longer, only navigate around a relatively small portion of the continent as a whole.

The point of most South America cruises is to experience Mother Nature, not necessarily to explore cities and towns like you would on a European itinerary. You'll see plenty of beautiful sights from your ship, but this is also a region where shore excursions are key to giving you the full experience.

A round-the-horn cruise will most likely take you between Buenos Aires, Argentina and Valparaiso (Santiago), Chile. The primary goal is to experience the natural wonders of the sparsely populated region of Patagonia, plus a little taste of Antarctica on the side. This includes the breathtaking Chilean Fjords, the majestic snow-capped Andes Mountains, glacier parks, waterfalls, turquoise lakes, deserts, white-sand beaches and endless scenic coastlines. When it comes to wildlife, you'll have a chance to see penguins in Puerto Madryn or the Falkland Islands, even if you don't veer off to Antarctica. There will be whales, seals, and a variety of fascinating sea birds as well.

One thing to prepare for, especially near Cape Horn at the southern tip of the continent, are rough and unpredictable seas. Even if you aren't prone to motion sickness, it's probably a good idea to pack a little seasickness medicine, just in case. Also, weather and sea conditions may prevent the ship from accessing certain ports-of-call during your cruise, with Port Stanley in the Falkland Islands being a rather common late scratch.

Other South American itineraries concentrate on the northern areas of the continent, usually sticking to one ocean or the other. On the Atlantic side, you might start in Buenos Aires, just like round-the-horn cruises, but head north to ports like Montevideo, São Paulo (Santos), Rio de Janeiro, Vitoria and Salvador. On the Pacific side, stops may include Pisco, Lima, Salaverry, Guayaquil, and Manta, with longer itineraries venturing up to Central America, Mexico, or possibly even through the Panama Canal. Small Ship and expedition lines are likely to stop in smaller ports that you have probably never heard of.

Cruises that focus on the northern end of the continent offer plenty of natural wonders as well, but here we are visiting populated areas with unique towns, cultures, people, and fascinating historical sites like Machu Picchu. I mention Machu Picchu specifically because it is not something you knock out with a shore excursion. This amazing, Mayan "lost city" should be a two or three-day land expedition that you add before or after your cruise, which would preferably begin or end in Lima, Peru.

Another cruise destination in this part of the world is the Galapagos Islands, off the coast of Ecuador, which is a bucket list item for many nature lovers and wildlife fans. That's because the creatures and surrounding vegetation here are nothing short of otherworldly. All ships follow a 15-day itinerary mandated by the Galapagos National Park, but the cruise lines often break it up into segments as short as four, five or eight days, which can alternately be combined into cruises of various lengths.

The Amazon River also falls into the South American cruise category because full-size cruise ships sail into it from the Atlantic. See **Chapter 15** for more details.

TIP: If you plan to take a round-the-horn cruise, make sure to pack for every conceivable weather condition from sweltering heat to frigid cold. Your ship will take you through a multitude of climates along the way.

South Pacific

Many people lump Hawaii into the South Pacific cruise region, but since Hawaii is a US territory, not to mention the primary or singular focus of so many cruise itineraries, the rest of the South Pacific warrants its own discussion.

The moment we hear "South Pacific", most of us envision the pristine beaches and crystal-clear waters of Tahiti, Fiji and Bora Bora—the perfect spots for a distant escape from the rest of the world, allowing us to recharge our batteries and rekindle romance.

But why do people take cruises here? Because there's so much more to see and do than just relax on the beach and frolic in the water. Cruises make it easy to meander from one island to another, stopping at ports that are neither bustling nor crowded. They also tend to be less expensive than land vacations, as the better resorts here tend to be pricey.

The islands scattered throughout this region of the Pacific are individually unique, too, and they represent a wide variety of cultures, customs, ancestral heritage and colonial histories. A cruise will provide you with a smorgasbord of satisfying tastes.

The South Pacific is particularly convenient to Australia and New Zealand, and many cruises originate from there. But a flight to Tahiti from the US West Coast isn't as grueling as it may seem. Tahiti is the perfect place to embark on a South Pacific cruise, perhaps with a land segment before or after.

Paul Gaugin Cruises offers year-round luxury sailings around the South Pacific islands on their aptly named *ms Paul Gaugin*, as does Windstar on the *Wind Spirit*. For the most part, both lines use Papeete, Tahiti as their primary port, often with round-trip itineraries to destinations like Fiji, the Society Islands, Bora Bora and others. Longer voyages include destinations farther out, like the Cook Islands. Paul Gaugin also offers the occasional 16- or 17-night cruise that ventures to Australia, Papua New Guinea, and even Bali, Indonesia.

Some of the major cruise lines stop at islands in the South Pacific, but it's usually in conjunction with a global repositioning, such as from Southeast Asia or Australia/New Zealand to Alaska in the spring, or vice-versa in the fall.

TIP: If you are taking a longer South Pacific cruise that sails to the Cook Islands, consider packing a seasickness remedy, just in case. The trip involves an extra sea day in each direction, and the ride can get a little rough, especially on the smaller luxury ships that typically operate here.

Western Europe & British Isles

Western European itineraries are those that span the distance between the Mediterranean and the Baltic, though many of these cruises will start or end in one of these regions. For example, you might begin your voyage in

Barcelona and end in London (Dover or Southampton), hitting Málaga, Gibraltar, Seville (Cádiz), Lisbon, Bilbao, Cherbourg, Paris (Le Havre), Bruges or Brussels (Zeebrugge), and perhaps even Amsterdam along the way.

In other words, the Mediterranean isn't the only cruise region with a multitude of European hopping-off points for fascinating tour opportunities.

Cruises around the British Isles give passengers a unique opportunity to experience its diverse selection of peoples, cultures, histories, landscapes and fascinating architecture on a single trip. Because of the numerous islands, their geographic arrangement, and the complications of traveling from one to the next, this would be a cost, time and logistically prohibitive venture if attempted as a land vacation, thereby making a cruise the ideal way to go.

When we refer to the British Isles as a cruise destination, we mean Great Britain (England, Scotland and Wales), Ireland, and numerous outlying islands including the Channel Islands (the Bailiwicks of Guernsey and Jersey), the Isle of Man (a self-governing crown dependency in the Irish Sea), the Inner and Outer Hebrides (northwestern Islands of Scotland), the Orkney Isles (northeastern islands of Scotland), and the Shetland Isles (a more distant, northeastern subarctic Scottish archipelago).

Most cruises circumvent Great Britain and Ireland, offering stops that take us to cities and towns at the top of our to-do lists such as London, Liverpool, Cardiff, Dublin, Belfast, Cork, Edinburgh, Glasgow and Invergordon. While they're at it, cruise ships often hit some of the above-referenced islands on the journey around, and may include a side trip to Guernsey in the English Channel (close to France) and/or a stop at Le Havre for a day-visit to Paris or Normandy. The longer the cruise, the more likely they are to expand your horizons, so to speak.

While it's possible to find cruises around Western Europe and the British Isles throughout the year, the season for most major cruise lines lasts from the spring to the fall. Exceptions are likely to occur on MSC, Costa and AIDA, which cater primarily to the European market.

TIP: Rain is always a possibility in the British Isles at any time of year, so be sure to pack an umbrella!

CHAPTER 4: CRUISE LINES

KEVIN STREUFERT

AIDA Cruises

Classification	Mass Market
Founded	1960 (as Deutsche Seereederei)
Headquarters	Rostock, Germany
Ownership	Carnival Corporation (NYSE: CCL)
Destinations	Worldwide
Ships	Small to Midsize
Languages	German
Caters to	German-speaking market, younger & otherwise active travelers
Known for	Sport and fitness offerings, club resort concept
Dining	Mostly open-seating, self-service, à la carte restaurants and specialty dining venues
Evening Attire	Ultra-Casual (no dress code)
Formal Nights	No
Slogan	"*Das Clubschiff*" (The Club Ship)

Summary

AIDA Cruises is geared toward younger or otherwise active, German-speaking travelers, offering a sports & fitness theme in a highly casual atmosphere. Even off-duty crew members are allowed to mingle freely with the passengers. Most oceanview staterooms include balconies.

Why Choose AIDA?

If you are athletic, speak German, and yearn for an easygoing cruise with an absence of uptight rules, AIDA may be ideal for you. Even if you aren't fluent in the language, you might be attracted to an immersion in the culture including the food, customs, a lack of typical North American inhibitions, and a super-casual atmosphere with the ultimate in flexibility. Programs with an athletic or health-based focus abound, and the spa is particularly large, offering an array of therapeutic relaxation spaces and treatments.

Azamara Club Cruises

Classification	Luxury
Founded	2007
Headquarters	Miami, Florida
Ownership	Royal Caribbean Cruises (NYSE: RCL)
Destinations	Europe, Asia, South America, West Indies
Ships	Small
Languages	English
Caters to	Affluent travelers from North America, the UK and Australia
Known for	Destination immersion, overnights in select ports, exceptional service
Dining	Main dining room with open seating, specialty restaurants, buffet venue
Evening Attire	Resort Casual
Formal Nights	No, but guests are free to dress up (common at specialty restaurants)
Slogan	*"Stay Longer. Experience More."*

Summary

Azamara is a small cruise line with three luxury ships holding 686 guests each. There are no current plans to add more. The line's focus is on "destination immersion", meaning more time and overnights in desirable ports to explore the area, including the nightlife. Though not considered by most travel professionals to be a full-fledged luxury offering, Azamara is still known for its highly inclusive amenities, personalized service, and shore excursions that focus on arts, culture, food and wine.

Why Choose Azamara?

Azamara offers an ideal entry point into the luxury, small-ship market with slightly lower fares and many inclusive amenities. Guests can expect a quiet, adult atmosphere with a focus on enrichment activities, food & wine, and an absence of children.

Blount Small Ship Adventures

Classification	Niche
Founded	1966
Headquarters	Warren, RI
Ownership	Blount Family (Private)
Destinations	American waterways, US East Coast, Islands of New England, Saguenay River, Caribbean, Cuba
Ships	Small
Languages	English
Caters to	Well-traveled, North American residents
Known for	Unique & less-frequented destinations, highly innovative small ships, American crew, BYOB
Dining	Main dining room only
Evening Attire	Casual
Formal Nights	None
Slogan	*"Small Ships. Big Adventures."*

Summary

Blount sails two, almost identical ships carrying only 83 passengers each. Both have unique design elements such as a retracting pilothouse and a shallow draft of just 66" that allows them to navigate through rivers and canals, under low bridges, and closer to shore. Beer and wine are served with lunch and dinner, but Blount encourages passengers to bring their own alcoholic beverages, greatly saving on the cost. Food is generally very good and reflects the locality. All crewmembers hail from the United States and are known for their super-friendly service, hence the large number of repeat passengers.

Why Choose Blount?

Given Blount's ability to access waters that most other ships can't, their cruises are ideal for well-traveled individuals looking to do something new and different. The low passenger count results in a very personal cruise experience with an absence of crowds.

Carnival Cruise Line

Classification	Mass Market
Founded	1972
Headquarters	Miami, Florida
Ownership	Carnival Corporation (NYSE: CCL)
Destinations	Worldwide
Ships	Midsize to Megaships
Languages	English
Caters to	Families, young adults
Known for	Fun/party atmosphere, great for kids, value-priced fares
Dining	Main dining room (open and fixed seating), numerous specialty restaurants (some included), buffet venue
Evening Attire	Cruise Casual
Formal Nights	Cruise Elegant – relaxed guidelines
Slogan	*"Fun for All. All for Fun."*

Summary

Carnival is the largest cruise line in the world and boasts the name of its parent company, Carnival Corporation, owner of nine other brands: Princess, Holland America, Cunard, Seabourn, Costa, AIDA, Fathom, P&O – UK, and P&O – Australia. All of these lines operate independently and have their own distinct cultures and offerings. Carnival (the cruise line) focuses primarily on 3 to 7-night cruises from US ports at low fares.

Why Choose Carnival?

When Carnival says they have "the fun ships", they really mean it. You can expect an ongoing party atmosphere in the adult areas and lots of entertaining activities for the kids, which drive a very high satisfaction rate with passengers. Carnival is also ideal for inexpensive cruise getaways, but don't expect posh staterooms or highly personalized service. That's not their aim. On the other hand, Carnival's quality and varieties of food can be surprisingly good.

Celebrity Cruises

Classification	Premium
Founded	1989
Headquarters	Miami, FL
Ownership	Royal Caribbean Cruises (NYSE: RCL)
Destinations	Worldwide
Ships	Midsize to Large
Languages	English
Caters to	Baby Boomers, food & wine aficionados, travelers with high standards for service
Known for	Luxurious contemporary décor, highly personalized service, gourmet cuisine, wine selection, dedicated suite class amenities: butler, lounge, restaurant, etc.
Dining	Main dining room with fixed and open seatings, specialty restaurants, buffet
Evening Attire	Stylish Resort Wear
Formal Nights	Evening Chic – relaxed guidelines
Slogan	*"Sail Beyond Borders"*

Summary

Celebrity Cruises offers a unique product in the Premium market segment with a near-Luxury cruise experience at a lower price level. Décor, highly personalized service, gourmet cuisine, wine selections, and the exclusive suite-guest spaces/amenities echo Luxury segment offerings, though base cruise fares are less inclusive than most Luxury lines. Ships have a clean, elegant feel with a focus on the finer things in life. The limited youth facilities and programs focus more on enrichment than entertainment, making Celebrity less appealing for families with younger children.

Why Choose Celebrity?

Celebrity is a great choice for affluent travelers looking for a quiet, upscale, contemporary adult experience without the lofty price tag of a Luxury cruise line. Those with high food & wine standards should be pleased, even outside of the suites-only environment.

71

Celestyal Cruises

Classification	Niche
Founded	1986 (as Louis Cruises)
Headquarters	Limassol, Cyprus
Ownership	Louis Group PLC (Private)
Destinations	Greece, Cuba
Ships	Small to Midsize
Languages	English
Caters to	North American, Swedish and other European travelers
Known for	Immersive cruises around Cuba, intimate Greek Isles sailings, affordable fares
Dining	Multiple dining rooms, but no specialty restaurants, although an upcharge menu is available
Evening Attire	Casual
Formal Nights	Elegant Attire
Slogan	*"Sea more."*

Summary

Celestyal Cruises out of Cypress has found success by focusing on two niche markets—Greece and Cuba. The line operates three older cruise ships that have undergone multiple refurbishments over the years, but still lack some of the up-to-date amenities and décor we've come to expect on other lines. Still, the accommodations are quite acceptable for the price, crewmembers provide excellent service, and the food can be very good. It's a great option for destination-focused, value-conscious travelers.

Why Choose Celestyal?

Celestyal's Cuba sailings, which circumvent the island nation and visit multiple ports of call (not just Havana), are generally considered to offer the most immersive and authentic Cuba cruise experiences in the industry. Likewise, its Greek Isles sailings provide an intimate connection to the destinations (which usually also include Kuşadasi, Turkey) and do so at an affordable price.

Costa Cruises

Classification	Mass Market
Founded	1854 (passenger ships in 1947)
Headquarters	Genoa, Italy
Ownership	Carnival Corporation (NYSE: CCL)
Destinations	Worldwide, but primarily Europe
Ships	Midsize to Large
Languages	Italian, French, Spanish, Portuguese, German and English
Caters to	European market, including the UK
Known for	Italian flair & cuisine, spa excellence
Dining	Main dining room (fixed and open seatings), specialty restaurants, buffet venue
Evening Attire	Resort Attire
Formal Nights	Yes, but relaxed guidelines
Slogan	*"Welcome to Happiness^2"*

Summary

Costa continues to focus on its Italian heritage in a big way, from wine and cuisine to ambience and décor—all part of its "Italy's Finest" initiative. While clearly aimed at the European market, roughly 10% of its passengers are from North America. Its upbeat vibe attracts a large number of younger travelers, though the passenger makeup will include retirees as well. The company offers numerous European itineraries such as the Mediterranean, Baltic and Western Europe, but also does sailings in the Caribbean, Indian Ocean, Middle East, Southeast Asia and South America.

Why Choose Costa?

Costa is a great choice for North American travelers who are multilingual, have European heritage, and/or enjoy mingling with passengers of various cultures and languages. For many, this would be a step outside their comfort zone, but that's what often produces life's most enriching experiences.

Crystal Cruises

Classification	Luxury
Founded	1988
Headquarters	Los Angeles, CA
Ownership	Genting Hong Kong (OTC: GTHKF)
Destinations	Worldwide
Ships	Midsize, Yachts, and River Ships
Languages	English
Caters to	Luxury market in the US, UK & Australia
Known for	Exceptional service, luxurious décor, extraordinary gourmet cuisine, extensive wine selection, high staff-to-guest ratio
Dining	Main dining room (fixed and open seatings), specialty restaurants, buffet
Daytime Attire	Resort Casual
Evening Attire	Crystal Casual (elegant casual)
Formal Nights	Black Tie Optional
Slogan	*"ALL Exclusive"*

Summary

Crystal Cruises prides itself on offering the finest service at sea and has carved out an enviable niche by offering a combination of small-ship Luxury characteristics and large-ship amenities and activities. Their ocean ships sit on the fence between small and midsize vessels, and they are constantly undergoing extensive upgrades and refurbishments. After its acquisition in 2015 by Genting Hong Kong, the line aggressively expanded into yacht sailings, river cruising, and "air cruises" on board a custom-outfitted Boeing 777.

Why Choose Crystal?

Crystal is perfect for highly affluent travelers looking for the pinnacle of service, cultural enrichment, gourmet cuisine and fine wine, all on an exquisite vessel offering more amenities than smaller Luxury-class ships.

Cunard Line

Classification	Premium/Luxury
Founded	1840
Headquarters	Southampton, England
Ownership	Carnival Corporation (NYSE: CCL)
Destinations	Transatlantic and Worldwide
Ships	Midsize to Large
Languages	English, German, French & Spanish
Caters to	Affluent travelers, Golden Era fans
Known for	Transatlantic voyages, British refinement
Dining	Multiple dining rooms with fixed seatings, specialty restaurants, buffet venue
Daytime Attire	Stylish Casual
Evening Attire	Informal (Jacket Required or Optional)
Formal Nights	Black Tie Optional
Slogan	*"Everything you wanted, nothing you expected."*

Summary

Cunard is the last remaining legacy line offering regular transatlantic passenger crossings, and they do so with British sophistication and style of the Golden Era of ocean travel. The line also cruises elsewhere in the world, either as world cruises or seasonal sailings from Southampton and New York. Cunard's ships strike a fine balance between modern-day amenities and the opulence of historic, grand-dame ocean liners.

Why Choose Cunard?

If you're looking for a cruise experience that echoes the golden days of the past with all the pomp and circumstance, including black-tie formal nights, afternoon tea, sophisticated entertainment, and impeccable white-glove service, look no further than Cunard. Their transatlantic crossings provide a fine alternative to air travel, if you have the time, with 8-day fares starting below the cost of flying business class. Many people fly out and cruise back, or vice-versa.

Disney Cruise Line

Classification	Mass Market/Niche
Founded	1995
Headquarters	Celebration, FL
Ownership	Disney Corporation (NYSE: DIS)
Destinations	Caribbean, Bahamas, Alaska, Europe
Ships	Midsize to Large
Languages	English
Caters to	Families
Known for	Top family cruise experience, Disney-themed atmosphere and entertainment, elegant ships, gourmet cuisine
Dining	Rotational dining experience at fixed seatings in various themed dining rooms, specialty restaurants, buffet venue
Evening Attire	Cruise Casual
Formal Nights	Dress-Up Night
	Pirate Night (and Deck Party)
Slogan	*"Happily Ever After...on the High Seas"*

Summary

Disney is the gold standard for families with small children, but it can stretch the budget. That's why many opt for Carnival, Royal Caribbean and NCL, all of which provide excellent youth programs of their own. When it comes to their ships, Disney creatively blends luxury and family elements, with features harkening to the ocean liners of the past. Shows, activities and onboard venues capitalize on Disney-owned mainstays like Star Wars, Marvel, Pirates of the Caribbean, Frozen, Mickey & Minnie, and a long list of others.

Why Choose Disney?

If you can afford it, Disney Cruises offers an over-the-top experience for kids while giving parents (and grandparents) a luxurious cruise voyage of their own with excellent service, top-notch cuisine, fine wine, and plenty of adult time while the kids remain occupied by engaging, well-supervised activities.

G Adventures

Classification	Niche/Expedition
Founded	1990 (as Gap Adventures)
Headquarters	Toronto, Ontario, Canada
Ownership	Private
Destinations	Antarctica, the Arctic & Norway
Ships	Small, Expedition
Languages	English
Caters to	Physically fit adventure-seekers
Known for	Expedition-type sailings, ecotourism, Antarctica camping, Jane Goodall Institute partnership, enrichment
Dining	Single dining room with one seating
Evening Attire	Casual
Formal Nights	None
Slogan	*"We LOVE changing people's lives"*

Summary

G Adventures is an adventure tour company with ocean and river expedition cruises on their list of offerings. They own and operate a 134-passenger ocean expedition ship, the *G Expedition*, which switches between Antarctica and the Arctic (including Norway) for the respective seasons. The ship has an ice-strengthened hull and plenty of expedition-type equipment including a fleet of Zodiac boats. Accommodations are modest, but comfortable, with all cabins offering an ocean view and en suite bath. Fares are reasonable and include all meals, excursions, an expedition parka (to keep), and the use of Wellington boots. Alcoholic beverages and gratuities are extra. G Adventures also offers Galapagos Island yacht cruises, sailboat tours for 9 people or less around the world, and small riverboat cruises for 30 passengers or less. All are ideal for group charters.

Why Choose G Adventures?

G Adventures is ideal for physically fit travelers seeking fun and active cruises and tours including Arctic and Antarctic expeditions.

Hapag-Lloyd Cruises

Classification	Luxury/Niche
Founded	1847 (as a shipping company)
Headquarters	Hamburg, Germany
Ownership	Multiple entities (Private)
Destinations	Worldwide, including Africa, Antarctica & the Arctic
Ships	Small, Expedition
Languages	German, English
Caters to	Affluent, German-speaking travelers along with the UK, US and Australia
Known for	Combination of cruise ships & expedition vessels, spas & spa staterooms, kids' facilities & programs, enrichment lectures
Dining	Multiple restaurants with open seating
Evening Attire	Informal
Formal Nights	Gala Nights - Formal
Slogan	*"We Make Your Cruise Dreams Come True"*

Summary

At first, Hapag-Lloyd was targeted exclusively at the German-speaking market, but they have made a strong effort of late to attract those who speak English, ensuring that onboard announcements and materials on designated ships are presented in both languages. A selection of shore excursions in English have also been added. The line focuses on luxury, excellent service, elaborate spa facilities, and providing in-depth enrichment lectures. Even expedition ships are more luxurious than similar vessels on other lines. Modern, upscale cuisine dominates the menus on board.

Why Choose Hapag-Lloyd?

Hapag-Lloyd is a compelling option for German-speaking travelers or English-speaking individuals looking for a more European cruise experience with all the unique food, traditions and cultural differences.

Holland America Line

Classification	Premium
Founded	1873 (Netherlands-America Steamship Co.)
Headquarters	Seattle, WA
Ownership	Carnival Corporation (NYSE: CCL)
Destinations	Worldwide
Ships	Midsize to Large
Languages	English
Caters to	Affluent, traditionally minded travelers
Known for	Traditional cruising experience with a respect for classic seafaring traditions, excellent service, enrichment programs
Dining	Main dining room with fixed and open seatings, specialty restaurants, buffet venue
Evening Attire	Smart Casual
Formal Nights	Gala Nights – Formal Optional
Slogan	*"Savor the Journey"*

Summary

Like Cunard, Holland America continues to respect its time-honored roots through ship design, nautical décor, and offerings such as afternoon tea, ballroom dancing and fixed dining options. After lagging for a while in the entertainment department, HAL has stepped up their game with B. B. King's Blues Club, Lincoln Center Stage and Billboard Onboard. Still, the average passenger age is older on HAL, particularly on the many lengthier itineraries.

Why Choose Holland America?

Holland America offers a high-quality traditional cruising experience mixed with modern conveniences at a particularly good value. Thus, it is a great alternative for people desiring a refined, sophisticated cruise vacation without paying the price of a Luxury line. For example, one can stay in a suite and dine in HAL's excellent specialty restaurants every night for half of what they would spend on a Luxury cruise for a similar experience.

Hurtigruten

Classification	Niche/Expedition
Founded	1893
Headquarters	Seattle, WA
Ownership	Private
Destinations	Norway, Arctic, Antarctic, Greenland, Iceland, The Americas, Russia, Alaska
Ships	Small, Expedition
Languages	Norwegian, English
Caters to	Norwegians & English-speaking market
Known for	Commuter transportation in Norway, destination immersion, sustainability
Dining	Main dining room and a 24-hour café
Evening Attire	Casual
Formal Nights	None
Slogan	"*World Leader in Exploration Travel*"

Summary

Hurtigruten's primary business is to transport passengers to and from the coastal towns, cities and islands of Norway, with scenic cruising being an ancillary business. Passengers are a combination of cruisers on the full one-way or 12-day, round-trip voyage mixed with Norwegians traveling from one place to another on a transient basis. Staterooms are modest, and entertainment is simple or absent except for the expedition teams on most ships, as the idea here is to let the remarkable scenery and wildlife keep you occupied. Expedition or cruise voyages to Antarctica, Alaska, The Americas, Iceland, Greenland and Svalbard (Norwegian Arctic Archipelago) are closer to mainstream, but still modest.

Why Choose Hurtigruten?

For North Americans, Hurtigruten offers something different, from destinations to the onboard experience. Those interested more in the unique destinations over being sumptuously fed and entertained may find Hurtigruten very satisfying. Northern Lights cruises are particularly popular.

International Expeditions

Classification	Niche/Expedition
Founded	1980
Headquarters	Helena, AL
Ownership	TUI Group
Destinations	Galápagos Islands, Amazon River, India, Cuba
Ships	Small, Expedition
Languages	English
Caters to	Well-educated, active adventure-seekers
Known for	Ecotourism, local culture immersion, highly active adventures
Dining	Varies by ship
Evening Attire	Casual
Formal Nights	None
Slogan	*"Discover Your True Nature"*

Summary

International Expeditions ("IE") is primarily a land-based tour company, but operates small cruise ships (ranging from 18 to 48 passengers) that explore the Galápagos Islands, the Amazon River in Peru and Ecuador (tributary), the Kaziranga and Brahmaputra Rivers in India, the Panama Canal, and multiple locations in Cuba out of Miami. They also occasionally charter ships elsewhere in the world. Sister companies are Zegrahm and Quark Expeditions. Ships, accommodations, dining arrangements and cruise vary, with the cruise portion sometimes being part of a cruisetour package. The emphasis of the trip is always on nature, wildlife, exploration, education, and interacting with the local people. Therefore, onboard entertainment is minimal.

Why Choose International Expeditions?

IE is a great choice for serious nature experts seeking a highly active, no-frills adventure in a particularly small group of fellow travelers.

Lindblad Expeditions/National Geographic

Classification	Niche/Expedition
Founded	1958 (as Lindblad Travel)
Headquarters	New York, NY
Ownership	Private
Destinations	Worldwide, including the Galápagos Islands, Cuba, Antarctica and the Arctic
Ships	Small, Expedition
Languages	English
Caters to	Well-educated, physically fit travelers
Known for	Expedition-type sailings, flexible itineraries (based on what is encountered), enrichment activities
Dining	Main dining room and bistro, both with open seating
Evening Attire	Casual
Formal Nights	None
Slogan	None

Summary

When Lindblad calls their cruises "expeditions", they really mean it. Then, when they partnered with National Geographic in 2004, it took things to another level. Lindblad operates serious vessels, many with reinforced hulls to navigate through icy waters. Their ships carry a plethora of exploration equipment from Zodiac boats and kayaks to hydrophones and underwater remote-operated vehicles (ROVs). Crewmembers are highly trained naturalists, historians and specialists who know their stuff and get you up close and personal with nature and wildlife. The company's small ships, with the largest holding only 148 guests, are nicely appointed, attractive and comfortable, but the focus here is on exploration, not sumptuous luxury.

Why Choose Lindblad?

Physically fit travelers seeking a true expedition experience with active engagement will love Lindblad.

MSC Cruises

Classification	Mass Market
Founded	1970 (Mediterranean Shipping Co.)
Headquarters	Geneva, Switzerland
Ownership	Private
Destinations	Worldwide (Mediterranean year-round)
Ships	Midsize to Megaships
Languages	Italian, French, Spanish, German, English
Caters to	European market, UK, North America
Known for	Mediterranean flair, low prices, unique entertainment, traditional practices
Dining	Main dining room with fixed and flexible seating options, specialty restaurants, buffet venue
Evening Attire	Informal (dresses/jackets)
Formal Nights	Gala Evenings – Formal Optional
Slogan	*"Masters of the Sea"*

Summary

While MSC Cruises still caters primarily to the European market, including the UK, their focus on North America grew in a big way when they homeported their extravagant new Megaship **MSC Seaside** in Miami in late 2017. A reasonably priced, all-inclusive luxury experience is available through their MSC Yacht Club with butler service and separate onboard facilities including restaurant, pool, bars, and lounge.

Why Choose MSC?

MSC offers a good value via lower cruise fares, though they are somewhat less inclusive. Still, this gives passengers the flexibility to add what they want and leave the rest. European sailings are a great choice for North American residents who are multilingual, have European heritage, and/or enjoy mingling with passengers of various cultures and languages. Cruises out of Miami attract a larger number of North American residents.

Noble Caledonia

Classification	Luxury/Niche
Founded	1991
Headquarters	London, England
Ownership	Private
Destinations	Worldwide
Ships	Small
Languages	English
Caters to	Mature British travelers
Known for	Social onboard atmosphere, unique itineraries and ports of call, cultural enrichment
Dining	Varies by ship
Evening Attire	Resort Casual
Formal Nights	None
Slogan	None

Summary

Noble Caledonia is a travel company that offers Small-ship and river cruises with a social, yacht-type atmosphere. The company says their onboard culture is "more akin to a country-hotel than one of the large ships trawling the seas today." This is an adult, house-party environment that is not suitable for children. The clientele is mature, primarily from the UK, and often represents a combination of singles, couples and groups of friends. Noble's ships are all chartered vessels from other cruise lines or sources. Two are operated full time by Noble—*ms Serenissima* and *ms Hebridean Sky*—while the rest are periodic charters of a multitude of different vessels, which means features and accommodations vary.

Why Choose Noble Caledonia?

Noble Caledonia is an ideal choice for British travelers looking for a small-ship cruise with like-minded upscale travelers in a highly social environment where it feels like cruising with friends. Singles integrate very well into their onboard culture.

Norwegian Cruise Line

Classification	Mass Market
Founded	1966 (as Norwegian Caribbean Line)
Headquarters	Miami, FL (Domiciled in Bermuda)
Ownership	Norwegian Cruise Line Holdings (NASDAQ: NCLH)
Destinations	Worldwide
Ships	Midsize to Megaships
Languages	English
Caters to	Young to middle-aged adults & families
Known for	Innovative ships, quality entertainment, contemporary style, upbeat atmosphere
Dining	Flexible "Freestyle" dining across the ship, main dining rooms, numerous specialty restaurants, buffet venue
Evening Attire	Smart casual
Formal Nights	Night Out and White Hot Party (flexible)
Slogan	*"Feel Free"*

Summary

Norwegian is one of the two most innovative cruise lines in the business when it comes to ship design, new attractions, onboard entertainment and specialty dining. A great example is the Waterfront, which turns the Promenade deck into a vibrant boardwalk of restaurants and bars with oceanside views. NCL offers a high-energy, exuberant atmosphere, evident from the venues on the ship all the way up to their corporate culture. Clientele is generally younger, active and mainstream.

Why Choose Norwegian?

NCL is ideal for younger or otherwise active adults as well as families looking for contemporary entertainment and lively onboard activities from water slides and rock-climbing to dancing and deck parties. Adult venues and activities make NCL perfect for getaway party cruises, and the award-winning youth facilities and programs will keep the kids highly entertained and safe.

Oceania Cruises

Classification	Premium/Luxury
Founded	2002
Headquarters	Miami, FL
Ownership	Apollo Global Mgmt (NYSE: APO)
Destinations	Worldwide
Ships	Small to Midsize
Languages	English
Caters to	Affluent adults from North America, UK
Known for	Great value, overnight port stays, enrichment activities, excellent service
Dining	Main dining room with fixed and open seatings, specialty restaurants, buffet venue
Evening Attire	Country Club Casual
Formal Nights	None
Slogan	*"Your World. Your Way."*

Summary

Oceania Cruises is known for its excellent value, with offerings similar to full-fledged Luxury lines at prices more comparable to the Premium segment. Airfare (at some level) is usually included. Smaller vessels allow Oceania to access and stay overnight in boutique ports that larger ships can't access. Entertainment focuses on sophistication and enrichment, from educational lectures and string quartets to jazz nights and Monte Carlo-style casino action. Oceania also focuses heavily on gourmet cuisine, wine and specialty cocktails. As with most luxury lines, the average passenger age is higher, and the lack of youth facilities and programs results in a limited number of families with small children.

Why Choose Oceania?

Oceania is perfect for affluent empty-nesters with interests in luxury, culture and epicurean cuisine at a particularly good value. The onboard environment tends to be highly social, so a desire to meet other like-minded individuals is a plus.

P&O Cruises – UK

Classification	Mass Market
Founded	1837 (as part of Peninsular and Oriental Steam Navigation Co.)
Headquarters	Southampton, England
Ownership	Carnival Corporation (NYSE: CCL)
Destinations	Worldwide
Ships	Small to Megaships
Languages	English
Caters to	UK Market
Known for	Cruises geared toward British tastes, celebrity chef affiliations, weddings at sea, family-friendly ships
Dining	Main dining room with fixed and open seatings, specialty restaurants, buffet
Evening Attire	Evening Casual
Formal Nights	Yes – Black Tie
Slogan	*"This is the life"*

Summary

The UK-based division of P&O Cruises is unapologetically geared toward the British market, but travelers from other English-speaking areas of the world are equally welcome. The line offers a variety of ships and sailings, some with an enthusiastic kid-friendly environment, while others cater to adults. Ship ages vary, meaning that some vessels will be fresher and more high-tech than others. Like most Mass-Market lines, many items are priced à la carte from alcohol and specialty restaurants to WiFi and shore excursions.

Why Choose P&O Cruises UK?

P&O Cruises UK is an easy choice for residents of the British Isles because of the commonality between daily life and the line's onboard environment, from cuisine to shipboard currency. Anglophiles from other areas of the world may find their sailings equally enjoyable.

P&O Cruises – Australia

Classification	Mass Market
Founded	1837 (as part of Peninsular and Oriental Steam Navigation Co.)
Headquarters	Sydney, Australia
Ownership	Carnival Corporation (NYSE: CCL)
Destinations	Australia & New Zealand, South Pacific, Southeast Asia
Ships	Midsize to Megaships
Languages	English
Caters to	Australia & New Zealand
Known for	Upbeat onboard culture, extensive kids' facilities & programs, budget fares
Dining	Main dining room with fixed and open seatings, specialty restaurants, food court venue
Evening Attire	Casual
Formal Nights	Party Nights – themed clothing
Slogan	*"Leave Earth for a while"*

Summary

The Australian-based division of P&O Cruises is the largest cruise operator in the South Pacific and is geared specifically to the Aussie market. Most ships in the fleet are repurposed, extensively remodeled vessels from other Carnival brands, such as the former Dawn Princess and both the *Ryndam* and *Statendam* from Holland America. The focus here is more on value than luxury, and like its sister brand, many amenities are à la carte, allowing passengers to pay for only what they use. Unlike most cruise lines, there is no automatic gratuity charge, so tipping is 100% discretionary.

Why Choose P&O Cruises Australia?

P&O Australia is natural choice for those who live Down Under. The line may also be appealing to travelers already visiting Australia and New Zealand who want to add a cruise component to their vacation, as P&O offers numerous options to choose from.

Paul Gaugin Cruises

Classification	Luxury
Founded	1998
Headquarters	Bellevue, WA
Ownership	Beachcomber Croisieres Ltd (Private)
Destinations	South Pacific
Ships	Small
Languages	English
Caters to	Affluent adults, couples, honeymooners
Known for	Exceptional service, cultural immersion, gourmet cuisine, casual atmosphere
Dining	2 main dining rooms and a poolside grill
Evening Attire	Island-Themed Resort Casual
Formal Nights	Tahitian Night (wraparound skirts, Polynesian shirts)
Slogan	None

Summary

Paul Gaugin Cruises operates a single 5-star cruise ship, the *m/s Paul Gaugin*, with just a 332-passenger capacity and all oceanview staterooms (70% with balconies). Cruises focus on Tahiti, French Polynesia and the South Pacific, with the occasional itinerary going as far west as Australia, New Zealand, Papua New Guinea, and even Bali, Indonesia. The ship is known for its first-class, intimate service and gourmet cuisine. Cruises offer an immersive experience of the islands and cultures with the help of prominent archeologists and marine biologists. Most passengers are middle-aged, but younger travelers and honeymooners are also somewhat common.

Why Choose Paul Gaugin?

Paul Gaugin is probably the most ideal and financially wise way to experience the South Pacific. Land-based resorts tend to be very expensive and less-inclusive, making a cruise the better deal, perhaps with a short land stay before or after. And, with Paul Gaugin's enrichment programs, you get a deeper experience.

Pearl Seas Cruises

Classification	Luxury/Niche
Founded	2014
Headquarters	Guilford, CT
Ownership	Pearl Seas Cruises, LLC (Private)
Destinations	Great Lakes, Canada, Caribbean, Cuba, Panama Canal
Ships	Small
Languages	English
Caters to	Middle-aged to older affluent North American travelers
Known for	Personalized service, large staterooms with balconies, destination immersion
Dining	Grand Dining Room with open seating at a single, fixed dining time
Evening Attire	Casual Resort Attire
Formal Nights	None
Slogan	*"Explore Well"*

Summary

Pearl Seas Cruises currently operates a single cruise ship, the **Pearl Mist**, with a modest 210-passenger capacity and oversized, all-balcony staterooms. The vessel's small size allows it to dock in numerous ports that are inaccessible to larger cruise ships, and the destination immersion is augmented by guest lecturers and local performers at the ports of call. The onboard atmosphere is intentionally slow and relaxed, with a lack of activity after 10:00pm. Passengers are somewhat older, and families are less common. The ship's décor has an Early-American flair with modern touches.

Why Choose Pearl Seas?

Pearl Seas is ideal for older North American travelers looking for a slow-paced, Small-ship luxury cruise experience close to home. An interest in destination immersion is ideal.

PONANT

Classification	Luxury/Niche
Founded	1988
Headquarters	Marseille, France
Ownership	Artémis (Private)
Destinations	Worldwide
Ships	Small (Mega-Yachts)
Languages	French, German, English
Caters to	Affluent travelers from France, elsewhere in Europe, and North America
Known for	French gastronomy and atmosphere, casual yacht experience, attentive service, excellent value
Dining	Two dining rooms with open seating
Evening Attire	Elegant, relaxed clothing
Formal Nights	Captain's Reception – Formal
Slogan	*"Yacht Cruises & Expeditions"*

Summary

PONANT offers a sophisticated mega-yacht experience with a distinctively French style and environment. Its small ships explore all seven continents and everything in between, particularly unique and exotic destinations that larger ships can't access. This includes expedition voyages to destinations like Antarctica or traversing the Northwest Passage. PONANT's fares generally offer a higher value than most luxury lines, although they are somewhat à la carte in nature. Its mega-yachts have no casinos, but do offer spas, a theater, pool, sun deck, lounges/bars, and two restaurants.

Why Choose PONANT?

PONANT is a great choice for travelers looking for a luxurious, intimate, European (particularly French) experience on an authentically designed mega-yacht with a relaxed, congenial atmosphere. An affinity for European gourmet cuisine and a good command of the French language would be helpful, although the crew will speak English.

Princess Cruises

Classification	Premium
Founded	1965
Headquarters	Santa Clara, CA
Ownership	Carnival Corporation (NYSE: CCL)
Destinations	Worldwide
Ships	Midsize to Large
Languages	English
Caters to	Mainstream to upscale travelers
Known for	Attentive service, fine dining options, expansive spa and fitness facilities, innovative features, attention to detail
Dining	Main dining room with fixed and open seatings, specialty restaurants, buffet venue
Evening Attire	Smart Casual
Formal Nights	Black Tie Optional (cruises of 5+ days)
Slogan	*"Come Back New"*

Summary

Possibly the most recognized name in cruising because of *The Love Boat* television series in the late 70s and 80s (shown daily on in-stateroom TV), Princess Cruises demonstrates a perfect blend of innovation and variety. The line's broad offerings allow it to cater to people with just about any travel tastes, especially those looking for a more refined experience than a Mass Market brand. While Princess doesn't focus heavily on kids, there are multiple age-based youth facilities and programs on board to keep those from 3 to 17 well entertained.

Why Choose Princess?

Princess is a smart choice for those seeking a more upscale cruise experience with fine cuisine options and cultural programs, yet still with plenty of mainstream entertainment. It is ideal for multi-generational family groups because of multiple offerings tailored for each age range and standard of service.

Quark Expeditions

Classification	Niche/Expedition
Founded	1991
Headquarters	Waterbury, VT
Ownership	TUI Group (Private)
Destinations	Antarctica and the Arctic
Ships	Small, Expedition
Languages	English
Caters to	Well-educated, physically fit travelers
Known for	Expedition-type sailings, flexible itineraries (based on what is encountered), onboard expert naturalists, enrichment program
Dining	Varies by ship
Evening Attire	Casual
Formal Nights	Captain's dinners (optional dress-up)
Slogan	*"The Leader in Polar Adventures"*

Summary

Quark is generally regarded as the frontrunner in Antarctic and Arctic expedition travel, using a broad fleet of chartered ships with ice-strengthened hulls. Its sister companies are Zegrahm and International Expeditions. Cruises feature extensive exploration equipment such as Zodiac boats, kayaks, scuba gear, and maybe even a helicopter. Some ships offer surprisingly luxurious accommodations including suites with balconies. Onboard entertainment is focused on enrichment and education. Quark's fares are somewhat à la carte, but include an official Quark parka for passengers to keep.

Why Choose Quark?

If you are interested in an otherworldly polar adventure, it's hard to imagine finding anyone better than Quark, with their well-equipped fleet and onboard experts. Many of their ships offer a good compromise between hard-core expeditions and luxury.

Regent Seven Seas Cruises

Classification	Luxury
Founded	1990 (as Radisson Seven Seas Cruises)
Headquarters	Miami, FL
Ownership	Norwegian Cruise Line Holdings (NASDAQ: NCLH)
Destinations	Worldwide
Ships	Small to Midsize
Languages	English
Caters to	Affluent, wealthy adults
Known for	Luxurious all-suite accommodations, highly inclusive fares, fine cuisine, enrichment lecture program
Dining	Selection of fine-dining and casual restaurants with open seating
Evening Attire	Elegant Casual
Formal Nights	Formal Optional
Slogan	*"The Most Inclusive Luxury Experience"*

Summary

Regent Seven Seas is known for providing exceptional, personalized service and being a truly all-inclusive luxury cruise line. This means all beverages (including alcohol), specialty dining, shore excursions, gratuities, WiFi, transfers, a pre-cruise hotel night, and a number of other items are covered. Even round-trip airfare at some level is included, so it's important to consider these items when comparing their cruise fares to other lines. The onboard culture is distinctively upscale, yet still relaxed and civilized. 98% of the all-suite accommodations offer balconies.

Why Choose Regent Seven Seas?

Regent is a fine choice for affluent travelers with high standards for service and luxury. One can expect attention to every fine detail and the staff's anticipation of virtually any need. Essentially, all dining venues on board are specialty restaurants.

Royal Caribbean International

Classification	Mass Market
Founded	1968 (in Norway)
Headquarters	Miami, FL
Ownership	Royal Caribbean Cruises Ltd (NYSE: RCL)
Destinations	Worldwide
Ships	Midsize to Megaships
Languages	English
Caters to	Young to middle-aged adults & families
Known for	Largest cruise ships in the world, cutting-edge industry innovation, high-quality entertainment, great for families
Dining	Main dining rooms with fixed and flexible seatings, lots of specialty restaurants, buffet venue
Evening Attire	Smart Casual
Formal Nights	Black Tie Optional
Slogan	*"Come Seek"*

Summary

Royal Caribbean's Oasis-Class ships are the largest in the industry (except the new **MSC Seaside**), and it's not unusual for cruise passengers to remain on board for the duration of their cruise because there's so much to do. Even on 7-day cruises, it's difficult to hit every onboard attraction and restaurant before it's time to head home. Kid zones and youth programs offer extensive activities and amenities. Multi-generational groups will find something for everyone, including the Suite Class experience for mature luxury travelers and the Dreamworks® Experience for kids.

Why Choose Royal Caribbean?

Royal Caribbean is a perfect choice for younger or otherwise active adults and families looking for over-the-top entertainment and an endless supply of things to do. All of its larger ships (not just Oasis-Class) are brimming with features and amenities, and there's a restaurant to satisfy every possible craving.

Seabourn Cruises

Classification	Luxury
Founded	1986 (as The Yachts of Seabourn)
Headquarters	Seattle, WA
Ownership	Carnival Corporation (NYSE: CCL)
Destinations	Worldwide
Ships	Small (Mega-Yachts)
Languages	English
Caters to	Affluent, wealthy adults
Known for	Exceptional service, luxurious all-suite accommodations, gourmet cuisine, exotic itineraries, social atmosphere
Dining	Choice of fine dining venues with open seating
Evening Attire	Elegant Casual
Formal Nights	Black Tie Optional
Slogan	*"Extraordinary Worlds"*

Summary

Seabourn Cruises operates small ultra-luxury ships that carry between 450 and 600 guests each, providing an intimate and highly personalized experience. Ships feel remarkably spacious, despite their size, like traveling on one's own yacht. All staterooms are suites with ocean views, and over 90% offer verandas. Itineraries are unique, often exotic, and include boutique ports larger ships can't access. Fares include most beverages as well as dining and gratuities, but shore excursions, WiFi, premium liquor/wines, laundry services and air travel cost extra.

Why Choose Seabourn?

Seabourn is ideal for affluent travelers seeking intuitive service, superb cuisine, luxurious accommodations, and an upscale atmosphere without pretentiousness. A social environment is encouraged, whereby passengers can enjoy interacting with other well-off, like-minded, seasoned travelers.

SeaDream Yacht Club

Classification	Luxury
Founded	2001
Headquarters	Oslo, Norway
Ownership	Atle Brynestad (Private)
Destinations	Mediterranean, Caribbean, Northern Europe, Asia-Pacific
Ships	Small (Mega-Yachts)
Languages	English
Caters to	Affluent, wealthy adults
Known for	Yachting theme, luxurious yet low-key experience, impeccable service
Dining	Indoor Dining Salon and al fresco Topside restaurant, all open seating
Evening Attire	Casually Elegant
Formal Nights	None
Slogan	*"It's Yachting, Not Cruising"*

Summary

SeaDream Yacht Club provides the closest thing in the cruise industry to a true yachting experience, with 112-passenger vessels designed more like private yachts than cruise ships, and a relaxed atmosphere akin to traveling with friends. While all staterooms offer an ocean view, none have balconies (much like a real yacht), but reflect a highly luxurious take on traditional nautical design schemes. Fares cover all cuisine, beverages (including premium liquor), and gratuities. Built-in marinas allow guests to utilize the yacht's collection of "water toys" while anchored. Sleeping under the stars on the topside Balinese dream beds is a popular feature.

Why Choose SeaDream?

SeaDream is a fine choice for affluent travelers looking for the closest thing to traveling on a private yacht—luxury, gourmet cuisine and exceptional service without the formality. Larger groups of family and friends may wish to charter an entire sailing, which is relatively easy given SeaDream's extra-small ships.

Silversea Cruises

Classification	Luxury
Founded	1994
Headquarters	Monaco
Ownership	Lefebvre Family of Rome (Private)
Destinations	Worldwide
Ships	Small
Languages	English
Caters to	Affluent, older, wealthy adults
Known for	Exceptional service, luxurious all-suite accommodations, spacious small ships, gourmet cuisine, exotic ports, expedition cruises, onboard enrichment lectures
Dining	Main dining room and 2 specialty restaurants (one with upcharge)
Evening Attire	5-Star Resort Casual and Informal
Formal Nights	Black Tie Optional
Slogan	*"Leader in Luxury Cruising"*

Summary

Silversea is known for its truly exceptional service, culinary excellence, attention to every fine detail, butler service, all-suite luxury accommodations with ocean views (most with balconies), and a clientele that exemplifies the highest socioeconomic status in the cruising industry. Passengers are addressed by name from the moment they step on board, and virtually every need is anticipated in advance. Fares are highly inclusive, with all beverages (except the highest premium liquors) and gratuities being covered. Expedition ships, for itineraries like the Galapagos Islands and Antarctica, are arguably the most luxurious in the industry.

Why Choose Silversea?

Silversea is an ideal selection for highly affluent travelers who demand the utmost in service, lavish surroundings and gourmet cuisine. Itineraries often include boutique ports with an absence of other cruise vessels.

Viking Ocean Cruises

Classification	Premium/Luxury
Founded	1997 (Viking River Cruises)
Headquarters	Los Angeles, CA
Ownership	Private
Destinations	Worldwide
Ships	Small
Languages	English
Caters to	Well-educated, affluent travelers from North America, the UK and Australia
Known for	Scandinavian décor, all-balcony staterooms, enrichment programs
Dining	11 dining venues, all open seating
Evening Attire	Elegant Casual
Formal Nights	None
Slogan	*"Ocean Cruising Reinvented"*

Summary

River cruise giant, Viking River Cruises, expanded into ocean cruising in 2015 with the introduction of the *Viking Star*, but the line is expanding quickly, slated to reach eight vessels by 2022 with an option on two more. Viking's 930-passenger ships are small but spacious, reflecting a contemporary but luxurious Scandinavian design scheme, and they're packed with large ship amenities (though casinos and kids' clubs are absent). Fares include wine & beer with lunch and dinner, specialty restaurants, WiFi, and a selection of shore excursions. Itineraries often focus on unique ports that only small ships can access. Onboard cuisine often uses fresh, local ingredients with selections that fit the itinerary.

Why Choose Viking?

For those with contemporary tastes and the desire for a more intimate cruising experience, Viking is ideal. Also, well-traveled people seeking new and unique ports of call will appreciate Viking's small-ship accessibility as well as the depth of their onboard enrichment program.

Windstar Cruises

Classification	Luxury
Founded	1984
Headquarters	Seattle, WA
Ownership	The Anschutz Corp (Private)
Destinations	Mediterranean, Northern Europe, South Pacific, Caribbean, South America
Ships	Small
Languages	English
Caters to	Affluent adults, sailing enthusiasts
Known for	Masted sailing ships and powered luxury yachts, excellent service, locally sourced cuisine, exclusive private onshore events, casual onboard culture
Dining	Selection of fine-dining restaurants with open seating, buffet venue
Evening Attire	Casual Elegance
Formal Nights	None
Slogan	*"180° From Ordinary"*

Summary

Windstar offers a selection of masted sailing ships and all-suite, powered mega-yachts that sail to desirable small ports and hidden harbors, with one ship sailing from Tahiti year-round. Its vessels carry just 148 to 310 guests and reflect a private yacht-like culture that feels casual and encourages socializing. The gourmet onboard cuisine is typically tailored to fresh, local ingredients. Fares are minimally inclusive, so you'll pay for alcohol, shore excursions, WiFi and gratuities a la carte—something to keep in mind when comparing fares across multiple luxury cruise lines.

Why Choose Windstar?

Windstar is a great choice for the discerning traveler who wants all the extravagances and culture of a refined small-ship cruising experience without the stuffiness. Its masted ships offer sailing buffs an extra touch of nostalgia without sacrificing luxury.

Zegrahm Expeditions

Classification	Niche/Expedition
Founded	1990
Headquarters	Seattle, WA
Ownership	TUI Group (Private)
Destinations	Antarctica, the Arctic, Europe, Africa, Asia, India, Australia, South Pacific, Alaska, Iceland, Central/South America
Ships	Small, Expedition
Languages	English
Caters to	Well-educated, physically fit travelers
Known for	Expedition-type sailings, flexible itineraries (based on what is encountered), immersion experts, partnered with The Nature Conservancy
Dining	Single dining room, single seating
Evening Attire	Casual
Formal Nights	Captain's Dinners (optional dressy)
Slogan	*"Beyond the Destination"*

Summary

Zegrahm focus strictly on expedition cruises using regularly chartered ships. Its sister companies are Quark and International Expeditions. Cruises feature the gamut of exploration equipment such as Zodiac boats, kayaks and scuba gear. Accommodations and common spaces are comfortable, but not frilly. Most cabins have an oceanview, but there are no balconies. Entertainment focuses on enrichment and education, with most excursions being nature-focused. Fares are mostly inclusive with all meals, beer & wine at lunch and dinner, tours & activities, gratuities, and transfers. Groups of six or more save 10%.

Why Choose Zegrahm?

Zegrahm is for travelers who are serious about exploring less-visited locales and not taking a posh cruise. Being physically fit is helpful with most excursions.

CHAPTER 5: WHAT'S ON BOARD?

KEVIN STREUFERT

Introduction

If you've read the previous sections on cruise line classifications and cruise ship types and sizes, you've probably surmised that cruise ships are as different from each other as they are similar. That means it's impossible for me to list what's on board your exact cruise ship.

Nevertheless, we'll look at the typical features of cruise ships in general, specifically within the Mass Market and Premium categories. Some of the information will apply to all cruise vessels, and some will not, but you should be able to draw some logical conclusions regarding what applies to your particular ship.

The Crew

Most of the officers and management personnel on a cruise ship are well-educated individuals from the United States and Europe including the UK and Scandinavia. Operating a large passenger vessel is a complex and daunting task, so these people are highly trained, experienced, and know what they're doing.

Cabin stewards, waiters, bartenders and housekeeping staff are typically from less wealthy nations including Indonesia, the Philippines, Malaysia, and other neighboring countries in that region of the world. They may also hail from South America or Africa.

In many cases, these people have left their families behind to work 6 to 8-month stretches of time to earn higher wages and provide a better life for everyone else. At the end of each assignment, they return home for a month or less before heading out into the world to do it all over again.

I try to keep this in mind as I contemplate if and how much extra money to tip those who provide extraordinary service.

> **TIP:** If you'd like to give a waiter or bartender extra gratuity for exceptional service, slip him or her a little cash near the end of the cruise. If you add extra to your drink receipt, it goes into the tip pool for the entire wait staff on the ship.

Main Dining Room

Your main dining room, of which there may be more than one, is likely to be a grand, multi-story venue with extravagant features that are intended to "wow" you when you walk in. Some look downright palatial with Florentine-capped columns and frescos on the ceiling, while others like Celebrity's Solstice-class ships will include a giant, glistening wine tower that rises to the ceiling.

Although the trend in the cruise industry is clearly moving toward flexible dining, many lines still provide an option to participate in the old-world oceangoing tradition of fixed seating times at dinner. You will probably see early and late seatings at 6:00pm and 8:15pm with the same table and wait staff throughout the cruise. This can be particularly beneficial if you're traveling in a group, as you have the comfort of knowing that all of you can dine together at a specific place and time on any evening, should everyone wish to do so. However, group members still have the option of dining elsewhere, if they prefer.

You'll also have the option of anytime dining, whereby you either show up at a dining room at your leisure, just like a casual restaurant on land (and potentially wait for a table), or make reservations to suit your schedule each day. I highly recommend making reservations, especially if you have a larger group.

Another time-honored tradition of ocean voyages is dining with people you don't know. If you're a couple, for example, you can choose to dine at an intimate table for two or sign up for a table of six or eight or more, where you'll be randomly seated with other passengers and have the opportunity to make new friends.

It's all up to you, and you can make those choices in advance. Just be aware that fixed seatings tend to fill up far in advance, particularly the early option, so you may be stuck with the late seating or anytime dining. Depending on your preferences, that may not be a bad thing, but it's always best to plan as far ahead as possible to get what you really want. When it comes to cruises, that's true with just about everything.

If you have special dietary concerns and didn't provide that information during your online check-in, make sure to inform your wait staff on the first night, and they will bend over backwards to ensure your needs are respected throughout the voyage. If you don't have the same wait staff each night or dine in other venues around the ship, just pass on your requirements to the new team. Cruise lines take dietary requirements very seriously and will make sure they're enthusiastically met.

> **TIP:** On cruise ships, there's usually no limit as to how much food you can order. Go ahead and get a lobster to go with that steak, four different side dishes when you can't make up your mind, or two desserts. You're on vacation! Just make a mental appointment to hit the fitness center early the next morning before you head on shore!

Specialty Restaurants

As discussed earlier, specialty restaurants can add an extra treat to any cruise, even if you experience just one of them.

This is not to say that food in the main dining room isn't very good. All cruise lines have stepped up their cuisine to the point where you'll rarely walk away feeling unsatisfied. But, there are unavoidable similarities to dining in a hotel ballroom during an event where vast numbers of people are being served by an institutional kitchen. In other words, attention to detail can't help but slip a little. Cruise line dining rooms are probably the best at maximizing food quality in such an environment, often hiring famous executive chefs to improve quality and taste, but there's a limit to what can be accomplished.

In the specialty restaurants, items like steaks, seafood, pasta and cultural dishes can be truly exquisite, as they are prepared in an intimate restaurant with a small kitchen. Here, the chefs are well-trained artisans turning out a relatively small number of dishes and paying attention to every detail. Ingredients are usually of the highest quality and authentically obtained from a particular part of the world, such as Kalamata olives, Parmigiano-Reggiano, extra-virgin olive oil, and Prosciutto from Italy for the ship's Italian specialty restaurant.

You'll receive more personalized and intimate service at the specialty restaurants, from the maître d' who greets you at the door to the waiters who attentively manage your table with precision and discretion. Think of a small epicurean restaurant or chop house in New York City where the service is almost as important as the well-crafted dishes that emerge from the kitchen.

The Buffet Restaurant

Every sizable cruise ship has a buffet restaurant, usually located near the top deck, not too far away from the main pool.

The place may seem like a zoo at first, but a strategic reconnaissance mission around the food stations will reveal that a choice meal can be assembled. Again, it's a matter of strategy, and I suggest forming a plan before "going in".

TIP: Don't assume you have to stick with all the selections on the pasta bar or salad station. Feel free to abscond with a meat item from a completely different section to add to either one, and create your own masterpiece. Then, why not add something "wrong" like a hot dog on the side?

Other Food Outlets

Most ships have a grill counter near the pool serving burgers, dogs, sausages, brats, fries and maybe even onion rings. If this is in the form of a free celebrity chef establishment like Guy's Burger Joint (Guy Fieri) on Carnival

Cruises, so much the better. If there's one with a small upcharge like Johnny Rockets on Royal Caribbean, there may not be a separate grill counter near the pool, but there will always be a place to score free burgers and dogs, and it's usually at the buffet restaurant.

You can also count on a pizza outlet with endless slices ready to go. It may be near the main pool or down on a lower deck.

Larger ships may have additional food and dessert options like a sushi bar, a wine lounge with wine-friendly snacks, a juice/smoothie bar, a spot serving ice cream and/or gelato, and even a cupcake counter. Some of these items may entail a small charge.

TIP: If you're racing to meet a shore excursion in the morning and want something delicious to grab and go, quality bakery items like croissants, pastries and muffins are usually available at the specialty coffee bar (see below).

Specialty Coffee Bar

If you have a hankering for an espresso, latte, cappuccino or other gourmet coffee beverage, this is the place to go. It will usually cost extra, but some unlimited drink packages cover specialty coffees in addition to alcohol and even bottled water. If you plan to have one or two specialty coffees every day, you should add that to your calculations in determining whether a drink package is a worthwhile up-front expense. Most people look at their folio at the end of their first cruise and shudder at how much they spent on drinks—particularly alcohol—and realize that the seemingly expensive beverage package would have saved them a bundle.

The specialty coffee bar usually has a case with complimentary pastries, croissants and other breakfast treats in the morning, transitioning to small sandwiches and other delicious snacks in the afternoon. These items are typically higher in quality than the buffet selections upstairs, making an enjoyable light breakfast or lunch.

TIP: Drip coffee is typically free on a cruise ship, and you can grab a cup to go at the buffet restaurant. But, some ships also have a self-service coffee station at the specialty coffee bar, and the quality of the brew is usually better.

Bars and Lounges

Alcoholic drinks are moneymakers for cruise lines, so it should come as no surprise that bars are in plentiful supply on a cruise ship. It is usually easy to flag down a waiter at places like the pool deck to bring a beer or cocktail to your lounge chair, again and again, even if you have an unlimited drink package. In the latter case, even though the cruise line isn't making incrementally more money each time they serve you a drink, they know you'll opt for that package on the next cruise if it's so easy to get what you want.

Bars sometimes offer small music acts or contests, but lounges are typically geared toward live entertainment, whether it's a rock or dance band, jazz trio, dueling pianos, stand-up comedy, trivia contest, or guest competitions like *The Newlywed Game, Battle of the Sexes,* and *Deal or No Deal.*

If you're interested in dancing, you may have several venues to choose from, with each offering a different genre of music. This may include a full-fledged disco with a DJ spinning tunes. See **Dance Club / Disco** later in this chapter.

Of course, each lounge will have one or more bars within it along with waiters ready to bring you cocktails.

Larger ships may offer additional themed bars or lounges focusing on things like sports, English pub drinks, fine wines, Champagne, or cigars. Royal Caribbean's newest ships offer their Bionic Bar, where a robot makes your cocktail, and their Rising Tide Bar moves between decks as you enjoy a drink or three.

If you're looking for a creative way (or an excuse) to drink, cruise ships are your answer.

> **TIP:** It pays to make friends with a bartender at the start of your cruise and consistently return to that venue for drinks. When things get crowded, and others are struggling to get the bartender's attention, he'll notice you in an instant and probably serve up "the usual" without even asking.

The Main Theater

The ship's main theater is used primarily for the evening's headline performance, entailing a "Broadway-type" show with dancing, singing, etc. In days' past, these shows were on the campy side, and some still are, but they've improved dramatically

over the past several years, as cruise lines have hired award-winning producers and writers, not to mention a higher caliber of performers. NCL and Royal Caribbean have even gone so far as to bring full-fledged Broadway musicals on board such as *Grease, Cats, We Will Rock You, Rock of Ages, After Midnight,* and *Mamma Mia.*

On occasion, a well-known performer or group act may serve as the evening's feature performance instead of a stage show. The *Blue Man Group* on NCL is a prime example.

The main theater is also used for destination talks, enrichment lectures (sometimes by world-renown figures or celebrities), and as a staging area for shore excursions and muster drills.

Most main theaters span two or three decks (sometimes even four) with an orchestra level and one or more balconies. Prime seating is often saved for suite guests and elite loyalty members.

TIP: Higher-end shows in the Main Theater, such as Broadway productions, may require reservations. Get the scoop and book your spots early. This may be possible online, in advance. Many people miss this requirement and show up at the theater, only to be turned away. You can wait until just before the performance, hoping for a no-show, but you'll end up with the worst seats.

Special Entertainment Venues

The larger the ship, the more likely it is to have additional entertainment venues, some of which may be outrageous, both literally and figuratively. One great example is the Aqua Theater  on Royal Caribbean's Oasis-Class ships (shown here). Performances are similar to Cirque du Soleil's *O* at the Bellagio in Las Vegas.

Holland America's *MS Koningsdam* has its Music Walk venue with three separate stages, offering simultaneous Classical, Rock/Pop, and Blues performances. Most ships offer an outdoor movie screen for watching movies with popcorn after dark, which was originally introduced by Princess as "Movies Under the Stars".

Other venues might include a second smaller performance hall, comedy club, movie theater, and/or a culinary arts studio for cooking demonstrations or classes.

> **TIP:** Like higher-end shows in the Main Theater, fixed feature-time performances in special entertainment venues may also require reservations. Make sure to find out and get yours right away. If they don't, arrive extra early to grab a good seat. If you get there 5 minutes prior to show time, you may not find any seats at all.

Dance Club / Disco

Most larger ships have a dedicated dance club or disco with a DJ spinning tunes until late every night. Depending on the "culture" of the cruise line, the place may be hopping or entirely dead.

For example, a disco on Royal Caribbean, Carnival or Norwegian—lines that focus on a younger demographic—will be livelier than one on Holland America or Princess, which tailor their ships for a more mature crowd. Super-premium and luxury lines may not have a disco at all, as they focus on empty-nesters and high-income individuals looking for a more relaxed experience.

If the ship doesn't have a dedicated disco, one of the lounges is often transformed into a dance club late in the evening. This venue will probably be located at the top of ship to prevent the noise from disturbing people in their staterooms who may be trying to sleep.

Pools

Most cruise ship pools are more appropriate for dipping than swimming, if not just providing a nucleus for chaise lounges, sunbathing,

socializing, people-watching, and partying. Oh, and there's the occasional water volleyball tournament, too.

Some vessels have multiple pools, but the real action and live music is centered at the main pool on the uppermost pool deck, close to the center of the ship. Other pools, such as those located at the rear, are for people more interested in relaxation than interacting with their fellow guests. However, it is not uncommon for boisterous individuals to be banned from the main pool, only to relocate to one of the calmer pools and stir up the atmosphere. Give it a little time, and they'll be moved on from there as well.

Some ships have spa and adult-only retreat pools, which offer the pinnacle of relaxation, and the chances of being disturbed there are slim to none.

Water slides are common on the larger, newer megaships, taking people down several decks to land in a splash area below. As time goes on, these slides get bigger and taller with more twists and turns. The largest one so far is The Abyss slide on *Harmony of the Seas*, plunging down 10 stories through the open area at the aft of the ship. As you may imagine, it is not for the faint of heart.

Most larger ships offer smaller pools and even mini-water parks for children, giving them a safe and healthy place to play and frolic in the water.

In cold or poor weather, the main pool may have a retractable cover to keep the party going.

Shopping

Shopping has evolved over time on cruises, and some ships now have shopping malls with chic boutique brands like Coach, Tiffany's and Bvlgari. These stores are mixed in with restaurants, bars, and maybe even an ice cream parlor or Starbucks.

Still, most vessels have a modest shopping arcade with a collection of boutiques owned and operated by the cruise line. One of them usually features jewelry and watches, while another will offer apparel and general sundries including cruise line-branded items. You can also count on a duty-free shop selling liquor, perfume, cigarettes, and skincare products. Note: "duty free" does not mean the store's merchandise is exempt from being claimed or isn't subject to customs duty when you arrive back in your home country, should you exceed your overall allowance.

There are two other caveats with duty-free shops. First, prices aren't as great as they used to be, and it takes a shrewd shopper to identify what's really a deal. Alternatively, if the shop offers a unique liquor that you can't get anywhere else (Macallan is notorious for creating delicious Scotch Whiskies to be retailed only through duty-free shops), that's another story. Be aware that any liquor you buy will be held for the duration of the cruise and delivered to your stateroom the night before your departure. You just can't beat the system.

Another common occurrence at the onboard shops is a promotion of the day, and you'll likely receive flyers in your stateroom advertising it. These can be for gold chains by the inch, watches, bracelets or other jewelry, and there will be tables outside the shops covered in the stuff. These usually aren't "sales", as the merchandise on a ship rarely changes in price from one day to the next. New merchandise usually appears instead. They don't want someone who purchased a watch on Embarkation Day to discover it's 30% off the final night of the cruise.

Casino

Almost all major cruise ships have a casino, and it's a big selling point for many cruisers. For fans of Vegas, it is often the deciding factor whether to take a cruise at all.

All the major games are represented from Blackjack and Texas Hold'em to Craps and Roulette, plus everything in between. Slot machines are also in plentiful supply including video reel slots.

Most cruise lines also have a players' club, just like a Vegas casino, with similar benefits. And, tournaments abound.

The minimum playing age is usually 18, but check with your cruise line to be sure. Gaming seminars for novice players are frequently offered during the day.

> **TIP:** If you enjoy gambling and plan to spend a lot of time in the casino, obtain a player's card and make sure it's swiped every time you play a game or slot machine. Like Vegas hotels, at-sea casino operators offer active gamblers exceptional fare deals to get them on the next cruise.

Spa

No ship would be complete without a spa. After all, soothing massages and other sublime body treatments heighten one's "vacation relaxation".

In addition to body treatments, some cruise ship spas are large enough to offer steam rooms, saunas and other relaxing spaces that can be used before or after treatments. If the ship offers spa-oriented staterooms, those guests are customarily allowed to use these spaces throughout the cruise, at their leisure.

Hair and beauty salons are also common and usually available for both sexes. They offer the gamut of hair services, manicures, pedicures, and even special treatments like teeth whitening. Just keep in mind that teeth-whitening can cause extra sensitivity to the teeth and gums, possibly affecting one's enjoyment of all the great cuisine on board.

On bigger ships, the spa may include a healthy dining venue with salads, smoothies and a selection of other "clean" and healthy foods.

TIP: Sea-day spa treatments are the most popular, so it's smart to reserve those online, in advance. However, book your *port-day* treatments on board after the spa offers discounts to fill up their appointment book. Alternatively, discounted port-day appointments may be offered online before your cruise, so keep an eye on those cruise line emails with special deals for your sailing.

Fitness Center

The Fitness Center is usually adjacent to the spa, carrying the same name, but may be in an entirely different location.

Most cruise ship fitness centers are sized appropriately for the passenger count and provide state-of-the-art machines in addition to free weights. They also offer morning group fitness classes from Yoga to Zumba, with the times listed in your daily newsletter. However, the classes may come at an extra charge.

Don't expect the cruise ship fitness center to be like a paltry little gym at a hotel. Cruise lines take these facilities seriously, especially since their guests are consuming more calories than they're accustomed to, and they need the workout. Don't be surprised if you walk into a facility that looks like a state-of-the-art, land-based health club. The larger the ship, the more extensive the fitness center and its programs will be.

Sport Court and Jogging Track

In addition to the fitness center, cruise ships typically include a sport court near the top of the ship for basketball, tennis, racquetball and other competitive sports. Some are even large enough for a full-court basketball game, and it's not uncommon to find the ship's officers out there in a friendly competition while getting their exercise.

You are also likely to discover a marked jogging track near the top deck, but walkers may find the Promenade deck more pleasant. There's usually a boardwalk that circumvents the ship, and sweaty joggers won't be speeding by every few seconds.

Other Sport and Recreational Facilities

Today's cruise ships offer a myriad of activities and recreational venues, with each new vessel offering something new and different. Most of them are even included in your cruise fare. Here are a few of the possibilities:

- Rock Climbing Walls
- Surf Simulators
- Skydiving Simulators
- Ziplining
- Ice Skating
- Bumper Cars
- Go Carts
- Miniature Golf
- Laser Tag
- Golf Driving Nets or Simulators
- Bowling
- Shuffleboard
- Ping Pong
- Video/Pinball Arcade

Spaces for Children and Teens

Many cruise ships have dedicated spaces for children and teens with specific age ranges for each. Some lines like Disney, Royal Caribbean and NCL take these to the extreme, providing over-the-top facilities and programs that keep kids safe and thoroughly entertained. They may not even want to go "home" with their parents at the end of the day—a tale I've heard more than once.

Expect a nursery for babies and one or more colorfully designed spaces for older kids with room for games, arts & crafts, and other activities. The primary focus is on "fun", though you'll find more of an educational or enrichment focus on Premium and Luxury lines.

While younger children are subject to supervision for their safety and entertainment, teens are generally free to come and go, utilizing their dedicated spaces for entertainment and socializing with peers. Teen spaces usually include video game consoles, air hockey, foosball, a dance floor with music equipment (or jukebox), and easy access to the arcade.

See **Child Care/Activities** and **Teen Programs** in **Chapter 11**.

TIP: Teens usually require a parent or guardian to sign a liability release for them to utilize the active recreational venues on board, so be sure you're there to help check them in.

Adult-Only Retreat

More and more ships have started offering serene, adult-only spaces like *The Sanctuary* on Princess or the *Solarium* on Celebrity.

These spaces usually include a pool and one or more saunas, but always offer plenty of comfortable lounges in a spa-type environment with discreet attendants ready to cater to your needs. Drinks, light snacks, hot or cold towels, and misting sprays are common.

The adult-only retreat is not just to separate oneself from children, who admittedly can be noisy. It's also for finding some peace and quiet away from the party scene at the main pool. It all depends on what type of experience you crave for your cruise vacation, or perhaps for the day, or maybe just for an hour or two.

Medical Center

Think of a cruise ship medical center as a cross between an urgent care facility and an ambulance. The doctor won't be performing any surgical procedures, but he or she can treat sprains, broken bones, a case of the flu, allergies, or any other ailment you would normally take to your personal physician or urgent care facility.

The medical center and its staff are also well-equipped to address trauma situations and stabilize patients, much like a paramedic in an ambulance, until ambulatory transport arrives to take the person to a hospital. If the ship is at sea, and the situation is critical enough, the patient will be evacuated off the ship via helicopter. For vessels with a helipad, this is relatively easy, but patients on a ship without a helipad will be raised up to the helicopter on a stretcher from an open deck.

Granted, medical evacuations via helicopter are not a frequent occurrence, but it does happen from time to time, as there is no way to predict when someone might experience a serious medical crisis. The hitch is that such evacuations can run $500,000 or more, and most travel insurance policies or major credit card benefits max out at $50,000 (if not $25,000). If this is of concern to you, ask your travel agent about a far more comprehensive third-party policy through a company like Allianz, which may cost the same or less than the cruise line options.

> **TIP:** Most health insurance policies do not cover medical treatment on a cruise ship or in foreign countries. At best, these expenses are treated as out-of-network care. However, most travel insurance and some elite credit card benefits will cover the difference. Do the research before you leave home to ensure you are properly protected.

Passenger Services/Guest Relations Desk

Think of the Passenger Services Desk on your cruise ship as the front desk of a hotel. This is where you go to replace a lost cruise card, resolve a discrepancy with your onboard account, change the automatic daily gratuity charge, obtain luggage tags for an earlier or later time on Debarkation Day, settle your account at the end of the cruise via cash or credit card, or resolve any other issues that may arise during your voyage.

If you are booked in a suite, you most likely have a dedicated onboard Concierge to handle these items, thereby obviating the need to wait in line here with other passengers.

The Passenger Services Desk also offers credit card cash advances, check cashing, and currency exchange services, usually via a separate counter. Some ships offer ATMs, which may dispense cash in multiple currencies.

TIP: Use your ATM card, debit card or credit card to obtain local currency at a major bank ATM on shore. The fees will be more reasonable, and the exchange rate from your home currency will include little or no premium. Avoid using ATMs provided by currency exchange companies at cruise ports or airports, which are usually located near currency exchange desks. These are merely a substitute for a transaction with a clerk, which means a transaction fee and an unfavorable exchange rate. Instead, look for ATMs at a bank in town or one that clearly displays a bank name.

CHAPTER 6: STATEROOMS

Introduction

Cruise ship staterooms can differ substantially in size, type, quality and configuration, resulting in more variations than a typical hotel. Most rooms in a hotel are of a standard size, but offer different views and levels of service,

with the rest being a handful of suites. Cruise ship cabins need to adapt to the design of a ship, resulting in all sorts of functional and design variations. The only thing we can state with certainty is that the majority of staterooms are SMALL. See the next section on **Limited Space**.

We can break down almost all stateroom choices into four primary categories:

1. Inside Staterooms (without a window or porthole)
2. Oceanview Staterooms (with a window or porthole)
3. Balcony (aka "Veranda") Staterooms
4. Suites

Cruise ship suites almost always have a balcony, unless it's a particularly small vessel with a traditional yacht design. The balcony itself will be larger than those attached to standard Balcony Staterooms, and the outside furniture will likely be of higher quality.

Mini-Suites may or may not receive the same perks and services as regular Suites. In terms of size and configuration, they are usually just larger versions of Balcony Staterooms.

Within each of the above categories, we can find a myriad of sizes, layouts and sometimes even premium benefits or services. On Celebrity Cruises, for example, there are two slightly larger premium Balcony Stateroom categories called "Concierge Class" and "Aqua Class". Concierge Class provides access to a full-time onboard concierge as well as typical suite-class perks like priority check-in, premium bedding, high-end bath amenities, and a lengthy list of other items. Aqua Class guests receive extensive spa amenities, a spa concierge, priority check-in, and their own "clean" restaurant called Blu.

Occasionally, you'll run across staterooms that fall outside the box. For instance, Royal Caribbean's Oasis-Class ships offer accommodations with windows or balconies overlooking their open interior venues like the Boardwalk (shown here) instead of the

ocean. RCL lumps these staterooms into their "Balcony" and "Ocean View" categories because the cabin layouts are the same, but in fact, there is no ocean view at all.

TIP: Take some time on the cruise line's website to review the various cabin options available on your ship of choice, then decide what's an absolute must versus what you're willing to give up if the price is too high. It'll make your life easier when it's time to make decisions.

Limited Space

When a new cruiser enters a ship stateroom for the first time, they are taken aback by how small it is. You can try to adjust your expectations by absorbing the square footage figure quoted online,  but the small size will still come as somewhat of a shock because online photos make cruise ship staterooms look bigger than they really are. People are accustomed to spacious hotel rooms, but cruise ship cabins are packed into a smaller area with the utmost efficiency, reducing the feasible dimensions.

Nevertheless, everyone adjusts to the size quickly. By day two of the cruise, it's hardly noticeable.

Suites on cruise ships are unquestionably larger, yet most aren't "suites" at all, just larger staterooms without a demising wall between the bedroom and living area. They're still not as roomy as a standard hotel room either. To get a true Suite, one must spend a multiple of the Balcony stateroom rate, but it usually comes with a long list of perks that help justify the cost.

TIP: If you've booked an interior stateroom and want to give it an Oceanview "feel", leave your TV on the bridge cam channel. You'll experience the light of sunrise on a real-time basis, and you'll have a makeshift nightlight at bedtime.

Bed Configurations

Most larger cruise lines outfit their staterooms with two extra-large/extra-long twin beds that can remain apart or be pushed together to form a king or queen, thereby allowing flexibility for different sets of travelers. You might expect a dip in between the two mattresses when pushed together, but that's rarely an issue. Cruise lines use a single mattress topper sized for the larger configuration, and they anchor the beds together securely. My wife and I have taken dozens of cruises together on many different lines and have never experienced an issue.

When you check in for your cruise online, there will be a place to designate whether you want the two beds linked together or split apart. Or, just inform your travel agent. If the beds aren't set up properly when you arrive, just tell your cabin steward. He'll fix the problem while you're at dinner that first evening, or perhaps when you're up on the Lido deck for the sail away party.

Third and fourth guests (and on rare occasions, a fifth) may be accommodated in a variety of ways depending on the size and configuration of the stateroom. If it is large enough to have a couch, that will likely be the convertible bed solution for passenger #3. If not, the cabin may have one or more  upper berths that fold out of the ceiling or wall, to be reached by a ladder like a bunk bed. These are most comfortable for younger, smaller passengers.

Your cabin steward will make up the extra bed(s) each evening as part of his turn-down service while you're at dinner. The next morning, he will put everything back the way it was, thereby providing as much living space as possible during waking hours. As we all know by now, stateroom space is like gold, so we need every square inch we can get!

TIP: If you prefer a soft bed, and yours is too hard, ask your cabin steward to add a mattress topper. Egg-crate foam pads or other cushy toppers are usually available.

Bathroom

Like the cabin itself, most standard cruise ship bathrooms are small (unlike the pictured example on the *Oasis of the Seas*) with a shower that is challenging to use if you are big or tall like me. Still, most are pleasantly designed and offer the essentials, including an adequate countertop and a reasonable amount of storage.

The bathroom steps up from the main stateroom floor to make room for plumbing, so be aware of that when you access the facilities in the middle of the night. It can be a delightful tripping hazard.

You'll notice that the toilet uses a vacuum system to flush, which significantly reduces water usage. You'll have to close the lid before pushing the flush button to help with the suction process.

Foreign objects can damage the system, so please don't discard anything other than toilet paper in there.

Light switches are sometimes located outside the bathroom, making it necessary to flip the switch and bathe the stateroom in light before you close the door. It's not the most pleasant experience for your cabin mate(s), but nature calls when nature calls. The designers of the latest and greatest cruise ships seem to have remedied that oversight.

> **TIP:** If you and your cabin mate(s) end up fighting over the bathroom or shower, you should be able to use the spa showers for free. The stalls are often larger, you'll have plenty of towels, and the selection of bath and hair products is usually better than what's in your stateroom.

Storage

Despite their space efficiency, cruise ship staterooms are still limited on storage, so I encourage my clients to avoid overpacking (see **How to Pack** in **Chapter 10**). However, there are usually a number of drawers, nooks, crannies, and well concealed cabinets to store extra items. Ask your cabin steward for help because there may be a secret compartment hiding behind a mirror or discreetly lurking inside a piece of furniture. But, when you pack up to leave, make sure to do a thorough search for your belongings.

One frequently overlooked storage area is under the bed, which will usually accommodate one or more empty suitcases, depending on their size. Otherwise, your luggage will take up valuable floor space or crowd all the clothing in your closet. Just be cognizant that cabin stewards often store your bedspread under the bed at turn-down (usually at the foot), thereby limiting the space somewhat.

> **TIP:** To save on room, store smaller suitcases inside larger ones before sliding them under the bed.

Amenities

Most cruise ship staterooms have amenities similar to hotel rooms such as a television, telephone, electronic safe, basic bath products (the quality of which varies by the price point of the cruise line and the level of cabin), a blow dryer, and in many cases a refrigerator. Just be aware that the refrigerator may be stocked with items that entail a charge if you consume them, just like a hotel minibar. It also means you'll have limited room to cool down the Champagne you ordered from room service or brought on board (see **Outside Wine/Alcohol** in **Chapter 11**).

Higher-end cabins and suites may include a myriad of other perks from bath robes and slippers to coffee machines and free alcoholic beverages. In any case, it's always a good idea to look up your exact cabin category on the cruise line's website in advance to confirm what's free and what's not.

Staterooms rarely have irons because they are considered a fire hazard. If you need something pressed, arrange in advance to have it done by housekeeping. Most cruise lines provide laundry bags and order forms where you can note varying degrees of urgency for an item's return, priced accordingly, so it helps to plan in advance. Clothing irons are also not allowed to be brought on board and will probably be removed from your luggage.

Power

All American-based cruise line staterooms provide standard 110V US power outlets, and newer ships tend to have them all over the place, including next to the bed. This echoes the same trend at hotels over

the last decade or so, driven by business travelers who complained that rooms were frustratingly short on power outlets—a valuable commodity considering all the gadgets we have to charge these days.

If you need to charge your cell phone, iPad, Bluetooth speaker and laptop at the same time, you should consider bringing an extension cord, multi-plug adapter or power strip, especially if you're traveling on an older ship. Make sure the adapter or power strip has a narrow plug because older ships may have recessed power receptacles that won't accommodate large chargers or plugs. Also, be aware that cruise lines generally allow extension cords and power strips, but they reserve the right to confiscate them if they appear faulty or are being used in a manner they deem to be unsafe.

Many cruise ship staterooms also provide one or two 220V European-style (Schuko) outlets, but if you need the UK or Australian configuration, bring an adapter. The only exception would be if you're traveling on a P&O UK or P&O Australia cruise, respectively.

> **TIP:** Bring a couple of US-to-European (Schuko) outlet adapters on every cruise, thereby allowing you to use the European-configured 220V outlets as well as the 110V US outlets. The chargers for most electronic devices (cell phones, computers, tablets, etc.) automatically adjust to voltages between 100V and 240V, so a voltage converter isn't necessary. Just read the small print on the charger itself to confirm that it complies.

Decorating Your Stateroom Door

Some people like to add a touch of personalization to their stateroom by decorating the outside of their hallway door, often to celebrate a special event. However, this is rarely done on premium and luxury lines.

There are even Facebook groups and Pinterest boards for cruise ship door decorating. If the idea excites you, there's no limit to the creative ideas you'll find online.

Feel free to be fun and creative, but don't use tape or stickers. Your cabin door is metal, so use magnets instead. The availability of magnetic decorations is abundant, and other items can be *held* to the door with magnets. Just make sure the magnets are strong enough to prevent items from falling to the floor each time the door is opened or closed.

The Suite Life

At first glance, cruise ship suites may seem overly expensive, especially considering the jump in price between a premium Balcony stateroom and a suite for a relatively small increase in square footage. Still, every bit of extra maneuvering space makes a surprisingly big difference, and suite passengers receive a long list of additional perks that help bridge that perceptual gap. If you've reserved a suite for your cruise, make sure to take advantage of them.

The perks vary from one cruise line to the next, but every suite guest should expect a speedy VIP check-in desk at the port, priority embarkation and debarkation, daily in-stateroom hors d'oeuvres, complimentary laundry services & shoe shines, an in-room coffee/espresso machine (or free & easy access to the same), priority reservations in the specialty restaurants, an upscale suites-only breakfast venue (if not an exclusive dining room for *every* meal), a larger bathroom with separate shower and bathtub, more closet and general storage space, and either a butler or a dedicated lounge with a concierge, sometimes both. Suite guests may even share an expansive dedicated space on the ship with its own sun deck, pool, hot tubs, cabanas, bar, lounge and a restaurant that rivals the top specialty venues on board. It's also possible for suite guests to receive an unlimited premium alcohol package and free WiFi.

Additional suite stateroom amenities often include premium bedding, higher-end balcony furniture, upgraded luxury bath products, fresh flowers, binoculars, umbrella, tote bag, a lighted make-up mirror, and many other goodies that vary by cruise line and suite category.

CHAPTER 7: HOW TO CHOOSE YOUR CRUISE

The Strategy

Let's return to the seven considerations listed in **Chapter I** when searching for the perfect cruise. While they are listed here in sequential order, one or two items might impact the ones before it, causing you to jump back and forth to make adjustments. That's all part of the process and gradually gets you closer to the goal. They are:

1. Region – where do I want to go?
2. Cruise Lines – who do I want to take me there?
3. Ships – what kind of vessel do I want to sail on?
4. Departure Port – how far will I travel to meet my ship?
5. Target Travel Dates – when do I want to go?
6. Itineraries/Sailings – what's available?
7. Stateroom & Price – what's the best room I can afford?

The first five items comprise your search criteria, and I hope you made plenty of notes on those subjects as you went through the first six chapters. Ideally, you've decided what appeals to you the most, meets your requirements, and fits into your budget. In other words, you should have a much clearer idea of what you're shooting for, and we're all set to put the pieces together.

Let's look at each subject individually, consider how it impacts the search process, and evaluate the best way to utilize that information to your advantage. Even better, we'll approach each item as its own step, leading to the final result as we wrap things up.

Region

Before we look at cruise lines, ships and available itineraries, it's important to select the general area or region where you'd like to take a cruise. After that, you should identify any specific ports, islands, cities or towns you absolutely must visit on your trip. Each piece of criteria you add further narrows down the choices, and you'll occasionally run into a situation  where it's impossible to meet every single requirement, thereby generating no results at all. For example, you may not be able to visit every destination on your list, and it becomes necessary to drop one or two. That isn't fun, but you can make a mental note to go there the next time around, right?

It's understandable if you haven't nailed down a specific region, but are stuck on a concept like "someplace warm and tropical". That doesn't necessarily mean generating so many itinerary choices that you'll feel like pulling your hair out. Just keep in mind that the process will take more time.

The region you choose will also determine which cruise lines you can select from, and you should consider which ones serve that area the best.

Cruise Lines

In the process of reviewing the four cruise line industry classifications and each line's unique characteristics, I hope you obtained a "feel" for which ones fit you the best. Most likely, you found two or more acceptable choices, but it's likely that a specific itinerary will determine which cruise line ultimately makes the final cut.

Just as we did with your desired cruise region, identifying your target cruise lines in advance will significantly narrow your initial search.

If you are working with a travel agent, he or she should have the resources to do a single search using a virtually unlimited set of criteria, targeting specific cruise lines, regions, included or excluded stops, included or excluded embarkation ports, and even specific ships. So, feel free to get as detailed as you like.

If you are searching on your own, it probably makes sense to search from the websites of each cruise line you have identified, though you probably won't have the option to narrow down the field with all the qualifiers I mentioned above. You'll need to do that manually while culling through the results.

Ships

Most cruise lines sail various types and sizes of ships, so it's a good idea to identify the ones you like and write them down. Or, at the very least, you can select the classes of ships you prefer within each line's fleet. Then, as you conduct your search and see the ship on each potential sailing, you can narrow down the field by rejecting the ships that don't meet your criteria.

To take this a step further, there are plenty of people who make the ship their top priority, with the cruise region and itinerary taking a back seat. That may sound odd, but here are two examples of where it makes sense.

First, let's say you're a couple who fell in love with a certain ship years ago, perhaps on your honeymoon, and it's a nostalgic treat to sail on her every year. If so, you'll check out her sailings, which hopefully change somewhat year to year, and book whatever's available to keep the romance alive.

The second example pertains to Megaships, which can be destinations on their own. There are many people who sail on Megaships, such as the Oasis-Class vessels from Royal Caribbean, and rarely (if ever) get off at ports of call because there's so much to do on board. Besides, things are less crowded when most of the other passengers are off the ship on shore excursions. In this case, one might restrict their search to the sailings of all four Oasis-Class ships and see what comes up.

Departure Ports

In some cases, particularly for cruises leaving out of domestic ports, it's helpful to specify one or more departure cities. Let's say, for example, you live in Dallas and would prefer to drive to meet your cruise instead of flying. That makes Galveston an ideal departure port, but you may be willing to go as far as New Orleans if there's an exceptionally attractive ship, sailing or cruise fare. If both cities are acceptable, add the departure ports of Galveston and New Orleans to your list of search criteria.

On the other hand, when it comes to destinations like the Mediterranean, restricting your choice of departure ports isn't such a great idea, as you'll eliminate some fantastic potential sailings. I would only consider this if you're already going to be in a particular country and hope to fit in a cruise at the start or end of your trip.

Let's say you'll be in Rome for a conference, wedding or family reunion and plan to take a weeklong cruise afterwards. If so, departing from Rome (Civitavecchia) would be ideal, but you might alternatively consider hopping on a train to Venice, Naples or Livorno. If nothing appealing shows up on *that* restricted search, perhaps it makes sense to broaden the parameters and consider a flight to Barcelona, Athens or elsewhere in the Mediterranean to catch a sailing that better suits your preferences. At the end of the cruise, you can easily fly home from the last port of call instead of going back to Rome.

Most cruise line website search engines allow you to specify one or more departure ports, so it's a qualifier you can easily add to your own search.

TIP: If you fly into and out of two different European cities from North America, airlines will usually price the fare as a round-trip ticket. You won't incur a penalty or be charged for two, one-way tickets.

Target Travel Dates

This leaves us with one last piece of search criteria: when would you like to travel?

It helps to establish a relatively large date range, if possible, thereby allowing you to see how cruise fares vary on different sailings (dates). The savings might be worth going earlier or later than you had originally planned.

For example, Alaska cruises generally run from May to September, but you'll see the highest fares in June, July and early August. If you are fine with the colder temperatures in May or September, you might be able to save a bundle by taking your vacation at one of those times.

Sometimes your dates are fixed, and there's no flexibility. Spring break and the holiday season are great examples. Just be prepared for cruise fares to be the highest at those times because of the greater demand. If you're thinking about a Christmas or New Years' cruise, for instance, the fares can be two or three times higher than for the exact same cruise earlier in December. It's all about supply and demand, just like everything else in the world.

Itineraries/Sailings (The Big Search)

Now that we've identified our criteria, it's time to feed it all into the best possible search engine(s) and see what comes up.

But first, let's clarify the difference between an itinerary and a sailing. An "itinerary" is the day-by-day schedule a ship follows during any sailing, whereas a "sailing" is an exact time period over which the ship *follows* that itinerary.

For example, many cruise ships follow the same itinerary over and over during their season in a particular region, which means they'll have numerous sailings of that itinerary. Let's say they depart on June 4, June 11, June 18, etc. In this case, you might say to your friends: "I'm taking the June fourth sailing on the *Norwegian Breakaway* to Bermuda this summer. Wanna come with?"

As a side note, there are quite a few cruise ships that follow the same itineraries year-round, which is fairly common in the Bahamas and the Caribbean. Another frequent practice is for a ship to follow *two* different itineraries, alternating them every week or ten days. For example, it might follow a 7-day Eastern Caribbean itinerary one week, a 7-day Western Caribbean itinerary the following week, and so on. That makes it possible to create a 14-day cruise by booking two back-to-back sailings. The only duplicate port of call will be your original embarkation city, to which you'll return in the middle of your vacation to offload one set of passengers and bring aboard the next.

If you've narrowed down your criteria to an ideal list, including your geographic region, preferred cruise lines, target travel dates, and maybe even a list of ships or departure ports, you'll end up with somewhere between 10 and 100 sailings to choose from. That may sound like a lot at the high end, but if you're using a large target date range, it will generate more results, and many of them will be the same itinerary on the same ship, over and over, as discussed above. Once you've seen it a few times, you can easily identify and skip it when it comes up again.

In fact, itineraries are probably the best place for you to start, as they are easy to digest and the fastest way to cut down the choices. Most likely, you'll have the ability to scroll through a list of sailing summaries that show the individual ports of call. If you don't like what you see, cross it off your list.

With the sailings you have left, bring back (or add in) your other criteria, such as your ideal dates and the types of ships you like, and evaluate how each sailing shapes up, especially compared to the others.

This is also a good time to compare prices, which should be clearly identified by cabin type on the listing of results. Of course, these are "from" prices, meaning that you might end up booking a more expensive category within that stateroom type to avoid an obstructed view, move to a higher deck, slide over to a better location of the ship, snag a little more room, etc.

At this point, you should only have a handful of cruises left, and you can weigh the pros and cons of each to make a solid choice.

As I mentioned earlier, a travel agent will most likely have the resources to perform a more sophisticated search and get to that final handful of cruises faster. Still, many people prefer to do their own online research and sift through the choices by themselves without the complications of involving another person. I totally get that because I've always been one of them.

However, allow me to suggest a hybrid strategy that I followed before becoming a travel professional. Go ahead and research everything to your heart's content, even to the point where you've selected a specific cruise. Then call your travel agent.

Here's why. Travel agents provide more value than just helping you select your cruise. They'll make sure your booking is done correctly and that you avoid any pitfalls like selecting a cabin that has obstructed views. Also, chances are they'll get you a better deal than what you see on the cruise line website, even if it's just a small onboard credit. In addition, a good agent will keep an eye on fares (up until your final payment) and grab any reductions for you on the spot. They'll also make sure everything goes off without a hitch, answer your questions, use their cruise line contacts to handle any problems, and make your life easier overall.

The best part about a travel agent is that their services don't cost you anything. Where else can you get so much help for free?

Just saying.

Stateroom & Price

We're down to the last component of your cruise booking, which is essentially how much you're going to spend.

Sure, you have a budget in mind, but there's more to consider than just the "priced from" cruise fares you see on your list of search results.

For example, there may be incentives offered with certain cabin categories such as an onboard credit, an unlimited beverage package (including alcohol), free gratuities, shore excursion credits, a specialty dining package, free third and fourth passengers in your stateroom (great for families), or even a spa treatment. You'll want to consider the value of these included items, if any, as you decide which category to book.

Let's say you're looking at a 7-day Eastern Caribbean cruise on a Mass-Market Megaship. The fare for an Inside stateroom is $895 per person, and an Oceanview is priced at $1,150—a difference of $255. However, booking the Oceanview stateroom qualifies you to choose a free perk, one of which is an unlimited beverage package that would cost you $455 if you purchased it separately. That makes the Oceanview stateroom $200 cheaper in the long run, assuming you would purchase the drink package anyway, as many people do.

In other words, look at the cost of your vacation as a whole, regardless of how or when you incur the costs, and game the system to ensure you pay the least amount of money overall.

The next and probably most important task is selecting your exact stateroom. First-time cruisers who book on their own are likely to choose the least-expensive cabin within their selected stateroom type, and that almost always comes with trade-offs. For example, the lowest-end balcony stateroom is likely to suffer from an obstructed view, a location near a noisy venue, or exposure to the stairwells and elevators. A cheap inside cabin may be frightfully tiny, share a wall with an elevator bank, or sit on the lowest possible deck, right above a smoke-filled crew lounge.

The easiest way to avoid any of these pitfalls is to work with an experienced travel agent who knows the ins and outs of cruise ships and has access to proprietary resources about every ship in every cruise line fleet. He or she can easily cull through the available staterooms for your cruise and steer you away from the ones with issues that might negatively impact your vacation. In the scheme of things, the difference in price from one category to the next within a particular stateroom type is typically minimal, so it's usually worth spending a little extra.

If you're still determined to book directly on the cruise line's website, here are a few suggestions to help you avoid disappointment.

As you look at the available stateroom categories and/or stateroom numbers for your cruise, look for a footnote, information button or drop-down box that might reveal extra details such as an obstructed view. Not all cruise lines provide this on their websites, but it's extra helpful when they do, and you can alter your choice accordingly.

Also, open up another window in your Web browser, navigate to the cruise line's website in that window as well, and look up your ship. Go to the deck plans, find the available staterooms (or color-coded stateroom categories), and evaluate their locations relative to other parts of the ship such as lifeboats, public venues on the decks above and below, stairwells, elevator banks, crew facilities (which may not be clearly marked), and any other ship components that might get in your way. Lifeboats along with all their mounting supports and equipment are the worst offenders when it comes to obstructed views, possibly including downward sightlines to the water or the pier from staterooms located immediately above them, so be careful to evaluate their position relative to the stateroom you're considering.

In addition to evaluating the deck plans, it may be helpful to look up a photo of the ship on the Internet to see how the lifeboats are situated relative to the Promenade Deck, which is used to access them in the event of an emergency. Sometimes the lifeboats are tucked entirely underneath the stateroom balconies above the Promenade Deck, thereby eliminating the obstruction issue entirely. But it's more common for them to be partially tucked in or just hanging off the side, thereby impacting the view of the staterooms closest to them—balcony cabins above and sometimes oceanview (window) cabins below.

I usually select the lowest-priced category within a particular stateroom type that does NOT suffer from any shortfalls, thereby eliminating as many as four lower-end categories. Higher-priced categories from that point are typically for "preferred locations", which may not be worth your money. For example, those who worry about seasickness will often pay extra for a stateroom at the center of the ship where the horizontal axis experiences the least movement. But, in reality, the difference in movement at the front or rear of the ship, where staterooms are less expensive, isn't as impactful as people think. If the forward staterooms are priced similarly to the aft staterooms, I'll choose a forward cabin to avoid vibrations from the engines at the rear when the ship navigates at low speeds in and out of port.

On the other hand, if you have any mobility issues, a midship stateroom relatively close to the elevators might actually make sense, as you'll have easier access to many venues on the ship. That being said, the main dining room is usually located aft and the main theater forward, so it's just about impossible to avoid a lot of walking on a cruise ship. But then, with all those extra calories to work off, perhaps it's not such a bad thing!

Getting back to those worried about seasickness, the vertical axis of the ship experiences the least motion on lower decks, but in this case, you get a price break. Ritzier cabins tend to be situated on higher decks where views are better, and staterooms are generally quieter.

Finally, if you're taking a one-way cruise that travels along a coastline, you should examine the route map and determine whether the land views will be better on the port or starboard side of the ship and book your stateroom accordingly.

Once you've chosen a great stateroom, it's time to complete your booking. See the next chapter for more details and recommendations.

> **TIP:** Just like airfares, cruise pricing can vary significantly from one travel week to the next for no apparent reason. If you have a little flexibility in your travel, try looking at sailings a week or two earlier and/or later than your target dates to see if you can get a better deal.

CHAPTER 8: BOOKING YOUR CRUISE

Booking Ahead and Monitoring Fares

The best cruise fares for the most desirable sailings are usually obtained by booking as far in advance as possible. Fares tend to start at their lowest point when a sailing is released—typically 18 to 24 months in advance—and gradually increase as

the ship fills up. Let's call this is our base-case scenario.

I usually recommend booking at least 12 months in advance, but if you can plan your vacation even further out, so much the better. Then, if the fare goes down between your original booking and final payment date, just grab the new deal. In almost every case, advance cruise bookings entail a refundable deposit, and the cruise lines are aware that you can cancel your reservation and make a new one at no cost. Therefore, if a lower fare shows up, it usually just takes a call to the reservations department, and they'll change your booking on the spot to save you the trouble of canceling and rebooking.

The impetus is on you to monitor the fares and make the call because they won't give it to you automatically. If you're working with a good travel agent, they should do all this as part of their service, thereby relieving you of the time and trouble.

Why would fares go down for your cruise, you may ask?

One possibility, though not as likely for a ship or itinerary in high demand, is that the staterooms aren't filling up as quickly as the cruise line had anticipated, and it becomes necessary to drop fares to attract more travelers. Like airlines, cruise line reservation systems have algorithms in place to evaluate the rate of bookings relative to anticipated velocity, and periodic fare adjustments are automatically implemented to help get those two factors in line.

The second and most likely scenario for a fare decrease is when the cruise line introduces a systemwide fare sale. This could last as little as one day or as long as several months.

Fare promotions of 24 hours to a week in duration will usually feature the best prices. It's a handy way for cruise lines to get their bookings back on track in a jiffy without materially impacting their bottom line via an extended sale. That doesn't mean a sale lasting a month or two won't result in a better deal than what you currently have, so it's always worth checking.

Some cruise line promotions don't entail a simple drop in fares. It could include free perks to save you money in the long run such as an unlimited drink package (including alcohol), an onboard credit, prepaid gratuities, a specialty dining package, shore excursion credits, or any combination thereof. If these freebies are items you would otherwise purchase on your own, that's money in the bank. It's important to do the math and see whether your all-in costs would be better or worse via the sale.

Cruise lines automatically notify the travel agent community about every new promotion, and a good agent will check every booking they have on that line to see if their clients can get a better deal. If it's a simple drop in fare, I grab it for my clients and email them with the good news. If it's more complicated than that, I give them a call to discuss the various options.

The only occasion where you may not be able to swing a lower fare is when your original booking entailed a reduced, non-refundable deposit. In that case, you may have to forfeit the original deposit and put up a new one. In some cases, the cruise line will overlook the fare rules and allow you to put up the difference. But if not, the lost deposit is another factor to consider as you compare the new and old pricing.

Barring the non-refundable deposit scenario, you should be able to grab any lower fares fare up until your final payment date.

After that, you're booking is essentially locked, but if you happen to come across a better deal just before you sail, call the cruise line to see if they'll give you the difference as an onboard credit. Sometimes they will, sometimes they won't, but it doesn't hurt to ask.

One other reason to book far in advance is to get your choice of staterooms, as the most desirable ones are snapped up first. This is particularly true of the coveted, oversized accessible cabins, which are always in limited supply and fill up extra early.

> **TIP:** If you book on your own, sign up for your cruise line's email list to be notified about new promotions. That way, you can reprice your cruise on the spot and see if you can get a better deal. Otherwise, you might miss it.

Booking at the Last Minute

Once upon a time, it was a "thing" to snag last-minute cruise specials, occasionally even on staterooms worth bragging about, but those days are essentially gone. Cruising has become so popular that the best ships usually book to capacity well in advance, reducing the need for cruise lines to drop prices at the last minute to fill up empty rooms.

You may have heard about people who wait until the final payment date for a particular cruise (usually 90 days prior to sailing), when a large number of prospective passengers will opt out and get their refundable deposits back. Theoretically, the cruise line will be left with a large inventory of empty staterooms, and they'll slash prices. After all, an occupied stateroom at any price is better than an empty one because it generates onboard revenue.

These days, cruise lines know how to manage the situation, and it's especially easy for the most desirable ships and itineraries.

More specifically, they oversell staterooms just like airlines oversell seats, booking passengers into "guaranty" categories after all the physical stateroom assignments have been taken. This means you are promised a stateroom in *at least* the category you've booked, if not better, giving the cruise line plenty of leeway for moving people around, granting upgrades to elite loyalty program members, and adeptly managing the empty space to accommodate the final passenger manifest.

Cruise lines can predict with a fair degree of accuracy how many people will "jump ship" on their cruise reservations, especially on the final payment date. While they may not be able to precisely peg those cancellations by each category, they can still manage the situation to where passengers are pleased with their final stateroom assignments.

This is not to say that last-minute specials are impossible to score. *Au contraire*, there are two scenarios where you stand a decent chance:

1. Off-peak travel periods, and
2. Ships or itineraries that generate less demand.

If you reviewed the cruise regions in **Chapter 3**, you probably noticed that each one has peak and off-peak periods. Cruise fares during off-peak times will be lower from the outset, but there's a decent chance those cruises still won't sell out, and last-minute deals will be offered.

For example, September is an ideal time to book a cruise to the Caribbean. The busy summer travel season is over, and most people (particularly families) are busy with school and getting back to work. Even the newest, biggest and most sought-after ships may have space left over. The same is true for May, just before the kids get out of school, and the summer season kicks off.

These days, it's difficult to find a cruise ship or itinerary that no one wants. Even older ships benefit from regular upgrades and refurbishments, making them entirely cruise-worthy. But newer vessels with their state-of-the-art amenities usually book up the fastest and at higher fares. In fact, if you go out and conduct a broad Internet search of all sailings over the next couple of weeks in your preferred region, you'll probably see the words "Call for Pricing" next to each cabin category for the best ships. That means they are essentially sold out. Still, there may be a few older ships with leftover cabins, possibly at attractive prices.

> **TIP:** Rather than culling through every available sailing for a screaming cruise special, call your travel agent or go to a reputable cruise travel website and find their "last-minute deals". These people have already done the research for you, and you'll have a selection of cruise lines and sailings to choose from. Even so, if you're hoping to score an unheard-of fare on the biggest, newest and coolest ship sailing the high seas...don't hold your breath.

Using a Travel Agent

My apologies if this handbook occasionally transgresses into a commercial for travel agents, but the industry is surprisingly misunderstood, and it has evolved considerably over the last decade or two. That means it's in everyone's best interest to get the real scoop, thereby allowing them to make well-informed decisions about how to book their cruise.

The most common misconception about travel agents is cost. After all, it's only logical to conclude that if you add another profit center into the cruise-reservation process, you'll end up paying for it somehow, whether it's a booking fee or a higher cruise fare, right? Well, as counterintuitive as it may seem, the opposite is true.

When it comes to most travel—and cruises in particular—travel agents don't cost the consumer anything. The travel provider (cruise line) pays the commission, and you get the agent's expert advice and assistance for free.

Why is that?

Because the vast majority of cruise bookings are already completed through travel agencies, so cruise lines price their fares under the assumption they'll be paying a commission. It's part of their normal cost of doing business. That means they're thrilled when passengers book directly on their websites and add that anticipated fee back to the bottom line. In essence, you are already paying for a travel agent's services through your cruise fare, and if you don't use one, you aren't getting your money's worth.

More likely than not, you'll also swing a better deal on your cruise through a travel agent. Those with larger agency networks may have access to a special inventory of staterooms that were set aside by the host agency a long time ago, often when rates were lower. Or, they may have access to an extra onboard credit that you can't get anywhere else. Even if neither of these benefits is available for your selected cruise, you will never pay more than the fare stated on the cruise line website, and you'll get a long list of services for free.

These services start with valuable expert advice throughout the selection, booking and planning process. Cruise vacations are far more complicated than airline tickets, hotels or even all-inclusive resorts because of the myriad of items to be selected, handled or addressed.

Less experienced cruisers tend to miss a few things, which can result in a disappointing vacation and a less efficient use of their money. This extensive handbook is a testament to how much there is to know and do.

A travel agent will also watch over your booking to make sure everything is done correctly and on time. He or she has the knowledge and industry resources and contacts to help you resolve problems quickly and efficiently. And, probably most important, you'll receive guidance on how to save money from the moment you make your reservation until the end of your cruise.

In total, a good travel agent will provide all of the following services:

1. Performing in-depth cruise searches through his or her extensive travel industry systems and resources;
2. Presenting attractive sailing options that conform to your personal tastes and budget;
3. Guiding you through the selection process from the sailing itself to your stateroom and every available option;
4. Making sure you receive the best possible pricing as well as any available credits, perks or incentives;
5. Completing your reservation thoroughly and efficiently, ensuring you avoid any issues with check-in or boarding;
6. Monitoring cruise-line promotions during your deposit period and grabbing any fare reductions or other perks;
7. Advising and assisting you with the travel documentation for your trip (including passport and visa requirements);
8. Providing guidance regarding the best shore excursions at your ports of call, available from your cruise line and reputable, alternative tour resources;
9. Cheerfully answering all your questions along the way;
10. Helping you resolve problems, including any mishaps that may occur during your trip.

TIP: Just like any profession, some travel agents are better than others. I recommend asking people you trust for a recommendation. Also, don't assume you have to choose someone in your city or state, as everything is done via email and over the phone these days.

Booking Online

I get it. Sometimes it's easier to do your own research, sit comfortably in your pajamas at your computer, and complete everything online by yourself. You don't have to involve another person in your vacation planning, and there's no waiting for information.

If you're a veteran cruiser who knows most of the "tricks of the trade", booking online can make sense. The only caveat is that you may not score the best fares and incentives, some of which are only available through a travel professional. Nevertheless, if you have the time and desire to keep on top of cruise-line promotions, researching them thoroughly to ensure you maximize every dollar you spend, you can still get a great deal. For some, paying a tad more is worth having complete control over their own booking.

If you do choose to book on your own, I recommend following the same process a good travel agent will implement on your behalf. Book your cruise as early as you can, which will most likely get you the best possible price, but keep an eye on fares and promotions to see if a better deal comes up. If so, call the cruise line's reservations department and ask to have your booking modified. This is something you can't do online because it will entail cancelling your old booking and making a new one. You'll have to charge a new deposit and wait for a refund of the old one.

162

As far as maximizing all the other details of your cruise, I recommend reading a guide like *THE Cruising Handbook* to learn all the best tips and tricks.

Wait, you already are! Good job!

Deposits, Final Payments and Refunds

Most cruise lines require a refundable deposit to hold your booking, with the most common amount being $250 per person. The remaining balance of your cruise fare is usually due around 90 days prior to sailing. Cruise lines vary on both items, so check to be sure.

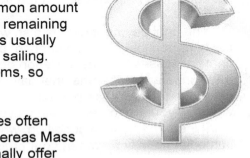

For example, Luxury lines often charge a higher deposit, whereas Mass Market companies occasionally offer reduced deposit promotions, which may be tied to a broader sale. But be careful. Reduced deposits may or may not be refundable, so find out before you enthusiastically charge your credit card, assuming you can get your money back if you opt out.

Non-refundable deposits may also prevent you from being able to modify your booking with a lower fare at no cost. The justification for cruise lines to willingly cooperate with fare reductions is that they know you can cancel on your own, get a refund of your original deposit, and create a new booking. In other words, it makes sense for them to get you to the same net effect without putting you through all the hassle of cancelling and rebooking. However, if rebooking on your own would result in a lost deposit, they may force you to take the same hit if they modify your existing booking with a new fare.

Also, be aware that modifying your booking with the latest and greatest promotion means you'll be subject to today's terms and conditions. For example, if you originally booked with a reduced,

$100 *refundable* deposit, and that special is no longer available, you'll have to post the difference for the new deposit. If deposits are back up to $250, that means another $150 per person. If your reduced deposit deal was ***non***-refundable, you may lose the $100 and be forced to post the full $250, though cruise lines are sometimes charitable and let you use the old deposit as a credit.

Once you reach the final payment date, it's time to cover the remaining balance of your cruise fare, which can be a big-ticket item for many. Sometimes, this is when we wish we HAD posted a full deposit to help spread out the financial burden!

The final payment date is also when you should purchase travel protection, if you so choose, because you'll be exposed to financial losses for a cancellation going forward. If you purchase travel insurance *after* the final payment date, you'll typically lose coverage for items like pre-existing medical conditions. In other words, if you are forced to cancel your cruise because of a worsened pre-existing condition, whether it applies to you or an immediate family member, your cruise fare won't be refunded.

All cruise fares are subject to cancellation provisions, usually consisting of a declining scale of refundability, gradually reducing from 100% the day before your final payment to 0% a week or so prior to sailing. If you have an emergency the week before your cruise and are forced to cancel, you'll lose all your money unless you have travel protection to back you up. This may be in the form of a purchased travel insurance policy or the cardholder benefits from a premium credit card. See **Chapter 18** for more details.

TIP: In the scheme of things, travel insurance is cheap, usually costing no more than the taxes on your cruise. Considering the typically large financial investment in a cruise vacation, it often makes sense. That's why travel agents are required by Federal law to offer it to their clients.

Stateroom Upgrades

When we hear the word "upgrade", we automatically think it's a good thing. That's because it usually is, especially with air travel. But when it comes to cruises, upgrades get complicated, and there are numerous factors to consider.

Let's look at the various ways an upgrade may come about as well as the advantages and disadvantages of each.

The first is an **Automatic Complimentary Upgrade** by the cruise line shortly before sailing to the next higher stateroom category, after which you or your travel agent will be informed of the new cabin assignment. In other words, you have no control over where they put you.

There's an outside possibility you'll be upgraded to the next stateroom type, like going from a standard balcony to a concierge-level balcony, spa balcony, or maybe even a mini-suite. But it usually means going to the same stateroom type in a "better location", as determined by the cruise line. You may or may not agree with their definition of a better location, but once the upgrade is done, you won't have the option of getting your old stateroom back, as they will have bumped you up to make room for someone else.

This may still be okay unless you're traveling with friends or family, and your new stateroom puts you on the opposite end of the ship, far away from the cluster of rooms you thoughtfully booked in advance to keep everyone together. Another potential risk is being switched from port to starboard, or vice-versa, after you strategically booked on the side of the ship that offered the best views during a coastal cruise.

If you are wheelchair-bound and currently booked in a coveted accessible stateroom, an automatic upgrade might take that away, thereby severely impacting the quality of your vacation.

Fortunately, you can avoid all of these risks and stay where you are by telling your travel agent (or calling the cruise line) to turn off automatics upgrades for your booking. I do this for people more often than not, as we have put so much effort into selecting the perfect stateroom and don't want to take any chances that the cruise line might "mess things up".

Upgrades may also come in the form of a **Discounted Upsell** offer at the last minute. This usually occurs when the upgrade opportunity results in a significant jump between the stateroom you currently have and the one being proposed—such as going from a balcony stateroom to a suite, or from a smaller suite to a larger suite. In this case, you'll be presented with the opportunity to pay a fraction of the going fare difference to put you into the nicer and larger accommodations. Fortunately, in most of these cases, you'll have the opportunity to evaluate the exact stateroom being offered and decide whether it's something you want to do before committing to the upgrade and additional outlay.

If you are offered an upgrade to a **suite**, it is very important to ask whether the usual suite amenities come with it. If it's a free upgrade, you'll probably take it no matter what, right? But if you're paying for the privilege, the value of all those perks plays a big part in whether you're getting your money's worth. For example, suites often come with things like butler service, a suite concierge, a dedicated gourmet restaurant, a suites-only passenger lounge (if not an extensive suite environment), free dry cleaning, daily hors d'oeuvres, fresh fruit, welcome sparkling wine, fresh flowers, upgraded bath amenities, robes, slippers, and possibly even a gourmet coffee machine. But the big-ticket suite amenity on some cruise lines is an unlimited premium drink package worth as much as $75 per day, per person. On a 7-day cruise, that amounts to $1,050 for a party of two, which could make or break the upgrade offer. If all you're getting is the extra space and none of the suite amenities, perhaps it makes sense to stay put.

It's also a good idea to check the going rate for the offered stateroom online and see how it compares to your original cruise fare plus the upsell premium. If the difference is minimal, and the upsell doesn't give you any suite amenities, tell the cruise line you'd rather pay the full difference in price for the suite and live it up like a king (or queen). Just be sure you aren't losing perks from your original booking that also have value such as onboard credits, prepaid gratuities, beverage packages, free WiFi, etc.

Again, I can't help but mention that a great travel agent already knows all this and will do the work for you.

CHAPTER 9: ACCESSORIZING YOUR CRUISE

Shore Excursions

Many people feel that shore excursions are the most rewarding part of a cruise because they maximize one's experience of a new destination. But before you jump online and book every cool-looking excursion in sight, let's take a deeper look.

First, not every port warrants an organized activity. If you're docking in a sleepy little European town where the port is within walking distance of everything, why not stroll around the place on your own, steal away some time in a sidewalk café, and enjoy the place like a local? You can even download a walking tour app to your phone and do an intimate little outing on your own for a fraction of the cost of a group excursion. See **Free Things to Do in Port** in **Chapter 13** for more ideas.

Second, cruise line tours aren't necessarily the be-all and end-all for shore excursions, despite all the efforts they employ to steer you away from other options. There are highly reputable and insured international companies like *Shore Trips*, for example, who offer tours that are usually more intimate and exclusive than the big-bus cruise line excursions, and they provide the same guaranties for an on-time return to the ship.

I regularly sign up my clients with *Shore Trips* to ensure they get our preferred pricing, then turn them loose online to search, explore and book whatever strikes their fancy. Most of them mix and match the cruise line tours and *Shore Trips* tours based on who has the best excursion option or price in each port. That's what I do on my personal cruise vacations.

There are also shore excursion vendors waiting at every port to serve willing passengers, but I caution my clients to be careful with this option. The matter of insurance and guarantees is thrown out the window, forcing you to make a judgment call. If it's a charming man with an E-Class Mercedes who promises to give you a tour of the area for $X and return you to the port a couple of hours before your ship departs, perhaps that's okay. I know people who've had a wonderful experience doing just that. On the other hand, if it's a collection of nefarious-looking characters with a rickety boat offering you a price that sounds too good to be true, it probably makes sense to move on.

When it comes to reserving organized tours in advance, whether through the cruise ship or a reputable third party, the best ones usually sell out early. Therefore, I suggest researching and booking your excursions online right after your final payment to ensure you get what you really want.

> **TIP:** Your cruise line may offer shore excursion discounts in advance of your cruise. Register online after you book and keep an eye on all those promotional emails between now and your sailing date. If you see a price drop on a tour you've already booked, cancel it and book again.

Spa Treatments

For many people, a cruise wouldn't be complete without the added relaxation of a massage or other spa treatment.

But when is the best time to head to the spa?

Sea days.

That means sea-day spa appointments fill up first, and by the time you step on board, all the best times may be gone. I recommend reserving your sea-day spa treatments online as early as possible, just like specialty dining and shore excursions.

But here's another option. If there's a stop on your itinerary that isn't particularly interesting to you, consider hanging back at the ship and enjoying a spa treatment while everyone else is on shore. Or, do a short excursion in the morning and spend the rest of the day back on board with a trip to the spa. The ship will be extra quiet, too, thereby enhancing your relaxation experience.

However, don't book those *port-day* appointments in advance unless the cruise line offers an online, early-booking discount. Wait until you get on board, and look for port-day specials intended to entice people to stay on board. You'll typically find these on a flyer stuck in your daily program. Otherwise, online reservations will be charged to you at full price.

Is it possible to get a discount on sea-day spa treatments? Not a chance.

Specialty Dining

It's true that you can take a cruise without ever paying extra for a morsel of food. You'll find complimentary dining venues and food counters on board that offer a wide array of delicious choices, so there's no reason to feel pressured into trying the specialty restaurants. However, if there's extra room in the travel budget, it's usually worth the splurge.

These venues typically include a steak & chop house, an Italian restaurant, perhaps an Asian-themed venue, and a host of other choices on larger ships. The per-person upcharge usually ranges from $25 to $50 for full dinner venues, while a specialty burger restaurant like Johnny Rockets on Royal Caribbean will run around $7.00.

If you do choose to splurge, I recommend booking your specialty dining reservations on the cruise line website as early as possible, especially if you're a couple traveling alone or with a larger group, as the smallest and largest tables fill up first. Yes, you'll have to pay the upcharge in advance, but you can get it back if you cancel within a reasonable period of time prior to your reservation, sometimes as late as 24 hours in advance.

Drink Packages

Unlimited drink packages offer various price points and combinations of beer, wine, spirits, soft drinks, specialty coffees, sports drinks and bottled water. The secret is to calculate what you think you'll consume during the cruise, do a little math, and see if one of these packages makes sense for you.

For those who drink alcohol, consumption levels tend to skyrocket on a cruise. First of all, you're on vacation. Then, you're immersed in a party atmosphere. And who wants to eat a nice dinner without a glass of wine…or three?

The alcohol packages may seem expensive at first look, but buying drinks a la carte can add up fast. Consider an average cost of $10-12 for each drink, multiplied times the number of drinks consumed each day, multiplied times the number of days in a cruise, not to mention glasses or bottles of wine at dinner, and it's not difficult to understand why. For many of us, an alcohol-based package makes sense.

By the way, if you're drinking all that alcohol, make sure to constantly rehydrate. I recommend making sure your package includes all the bottled water you can drink and downing one of those small bottles for each alcoholic beverage. You'll feel a lot better the next morning and be more interested in drinking the next day, thereby getting your money's worth.

Drink packages are one thing you don't have to buy in advance because they don't sell out. Feel free to save it for your onboard account, especially if your cruise deal included an onboard credit. You have to spend that money on something, right? Usually, any bartender can add the drink package to your account and put the corresponding sticker on your cruise card in less than a minute. Alternatively, check with the front desk, your butler or the concierge, if applicable.

> **TIP:** Your cruise line may offer drink package discounts in advance of your cruise, which is another good reason to register online right after booking and keep an eye on all those promotional emails. If this happens, it makes more sense to buy the package in advance.

Internet / WiFi Packages

The speed and reliability of Internet service on cruise ships gets better all the time, especially with newer vessels, but the WiFi on many cruise ships is still slow and inconsistent. Still, some people can't afford to be completely out of touch, so we do the best with what's available.

Depending on the cruise line, you may be offered Internet/WiFi plans with a stated number of minutes, but more and more ships are offering unlimited options at a fixed daily price. Just like drink packages, the Internet won't sell out, so this is another amenity you can book on board, if you like. Just keep an eye out for those online specials before you leave home.

If you buy an unlimited Internet package online, you'll pay for service over the entire cruise, whereas you can wait for a day or two after boarding the ship to start the service and only pay for the *remainder* of the cruise. This cost-saving strategy is particularly helpful if you don't mind being out of touch for a little while, but eventually want to catch up on emails and such when it makes sense.

One thing **everyone** should do before boarding a cruise ship is to turn off DATA ROAMING on their cell phones. In the event you use the ship's WiFi for Internet on your phone, and you inadvertently lose the WiFi connection while surfing, emailing, etc., you don't want your phone to switch over to the ship's cellular service for data, which will cost a small fortune.

Some people put their phones in airplane mode and switch on WiFi for the duration of their cruise, which also works fine. You won't receive any phone calls or standard SMS texts, but that will work just fine if you tell people in advance that you can only be reached via email. You may also be able to receive texts if you use a WiFi-based app like Apple iMessage, WhatsApp or Tango. These alternative messaging options are also a great way for groups to communicate with each other while on board ship, assuming everyone signs up for unlimited WiFi. You may also be able to use the cruise line's Onboard App to communicate with each other, if one is available on your cruise (see **Chapter 12**).

If you need to be reachable by phone while you're away, it's fine to simply turn off data roaming and leave your cell service active. Just check your Caller ID each time your phone rings to decide whether to incur the high per-minute charges or let the call go to voicemail. You may also receive texts, but most cellular carriers only charge for *sent* texts, not received texts. Still, it's a good idea to check with your provider to be sure.

I recommend turning off data roaming whenever my clients travel outside the country, be it on a cruise or otherwise, unless they have an international cellular data plan (see the next section). Otherwise, data roaming charges can amount to hundreds or thousands of dollars in just a few days. If you have an emergency overseas and need to check emails or use the Web, try to find the closest public WiFi, Starbucks or other business with free Internet. If that's impossible, switch on data roaming, do your business quickly, and shut it back off. Still, just doing that can rack up a ton of charges from hours or days of emails streaming to your phone.

> **TIP:** WiFi packages are usually purchased for "one device", but in most cases, this really means "one device at a time". Therefore, if you don't need WiFi to be active 24/7 on your phone, feel free to share it with your other devices or cabin mate(s) by logging out one device and logging in the next.

Cruise Ship Plan from Your Cell Carrier

Almost all cruise ships provide cellular phone service after they have reached a certain distance from shore (typically 12 nautical miles) via a provider like Wireless Maritime Services. Unless you buy a cruise ship service plan in advance from your home cellular provider, the per minute rates using the onboard system (via cellular roaming) are very expensive. But, if you're looking forward to being out of touch for a while, you may not care, as the only time you'll use it is during an emergency.

Your cell phone will most likely log on to the ship's cellular service automatically after it has been activated, but you won't incur any charges unless you accept or make a phone call. In other words, you can check your caller ID for any incoming calls and simply ignore those for which the exorbitant charges aren't worthwhile. You may also receive texts, but most cellular carriers only charge for *sent* messages, not received messages. Still, it's smart to check with your carrier to be sure and get the per-minute cruise ship rates while you're at it.

Cruise ship cellular service plans are similar to international cellular plans, offering voice, text and data allotments. However, the two types of plans are usually not interchangeable. In other words, you'll need to make different arrangements for calls, texts and data on the ship versus on shore in a foreign country or territory.

Gifts for Cruise Travelers

If you'd like to buy a gift for someone on a cruise, whether you're staying at home or traveling with them, you can do so on the cruise line's website. Maybe you'd like to arrange for a little surprise to be waiting for a loved one in their stateroom as they head off on a birthday cruise. Or, perhaps you're the organizer of a family or group trip and plan to provide a special bon voyage treat for everyone. Gifts range from simple cupcakes to bottles of wine to a full-fledged decoration package for a birthday, anniversary, wedding or honeymoon.

Every cruise line website is different, so it may take a little searching. The gift section is usually located in an area for passengers who have already booked their cruise. For example, Royal Caribbean's website has a button at the top of their main webpage that says, "Already Booked". Once you hover over it, you can click on "Royal Gifts" and start shopping. On Carnival, you simply hover over the "Manage" button and select "In-Room Gifts & Shopping".

To ensure a successful delivery, you need the name of the ship, the sailing date, and the name of one of the passengers EXACTLY as it appears in the cruise line's reservation system. Your safest bet is to have the booking number, even though it may be a challenge to obtain it secretly, assuming you want the gift to be a surprise.

KEVIN STREUFERT

CHAPTER 10: PREPARING FOR YOUR CRUISE

Passports and Visas

The first thing I do after booking a cruise or international trip for a client is to implore them, probably to the point of being annoying, to ensure their passports are in order.

Long gone are the days when you could travel to Mexico, the Caribbean or Canada with just a driver's license or a birth certificate. In addition, almost every country in the world requires your passport to expire at least six months after the conclusion of your trip, meaning that a passport becomes intrinsically useless six months prior to its expiration date. It is critical to do that calculation right now and see if you're okay.

Start your passport application or renewal as early as possible. The US State Department usually runs 4 to 6 weeks for processing, but what if there's a glitch with your application that requires added time to resolve? New and renewal passport backlogs also come in waves, peaking after the first of the year and just before the busy summer travel season. You'll also see spikes in response to developments like the Real ID Act. Sure, you can expedite the process via mail or even faster in person at a passport office, but why incur the added expense and stress?

If you are only planning to travel to and from Canada, Mexico, the Caribbean or Bermuda, you might be tempted to save a few dollars by applying for the less expensive US Passport Card. However, this card is only valid for land border crossings and sea ports, **not for travel by air**. That means if your cruise starts in Vancouver, you won't be able to fly there. You'll have to drive or take a bus across the border instead. I suggest spending the few extra bucks for a full-fledged passport, if not both documents if you frequently cross land borders with Mexico and/or Canada, and take all the variables out of the picture.

If you're taking an Alaska cruise out of Seattle, please don't assume a passport isn't required. Yes, Alaska is part of the USA, but Alaska cruises will stop in Victoria, BC or another Canadian port because of a US law prohibiting foreign-flagged vessels (almost all cruise ships) from sailing US-only itineraries. People sometimes think they can resolve the problem by staying on the ship in Canadian ports, but the cruise line is required by international law to ensure that every passenger boarding the ship has the requisite documents to disembark in every port of call.

In other words, if you don't have a passport with the six-month expiration cushion, you won't be allowed to board. It happens to hundreds of passengers in Seattle every year.

To add insult to injury, the cruise line won't refund your fare if you're missing any required travel documents. Likewise, travel insurance won't cover a passenger's own negligence, which is applicable in these cases.

Now you understand why I make such a big deal about passports.

Visas are another animal altogether. Most countries to which Americans travel do not require visas, but once you venture to Eastern Europe, the former Soviet Republics and Asia, visas are often compulsory. That being said, it doesn't necessarily mean you need a visa if you arrive on a cruise ship.

In most cases, if you're taking an organized tour, these countries will consider your tour guide a living, breathing visa. Their governments are aware that you will be spending the day on shore in a controlled group and returning to your cruise ship for the night, even if the vessel is scheduled to stay in port for several days. This is often the case in St. Petersburg, Russia.

However, if you're planning to venture out on your own in Russia, you'll need to obtain a visa from that country's local consulate in the US at least a week or two in advance. In some cases, like Russia, you'll also need an immigration card. Be sure to keep close track of those documents while you're out and about because Russian immigration will not let you back on the ship without them. Even worse, they have been known to arrest, detain and levy thousands of dollars in fines to American tourists who lose their travel documents. Please don't let that happen to you.

I always discuss documentation requirements with my clients and make sure they have what they need. If you have any doubts whatsoever, call your travel agent or the cruise line. It's better to be safe than sorry.

> **TIP:** Make two copies of your passport's biodata page and leave one copy with family or a friend back home. Carry the other with you in case your passport is lost or stolen. It won't act as a replacement, but will help expedite obtaining a new one at the nearest US Embassy or Consulate. If your copy goes missing, the friend or family member can fax or email it to you or the proper authorities. It is equally helpful to take a picture of the biodata page with your cell phone.

Online Check-In

Cruise lines usually require passengers to check in online at least 3 days prior to the sailing date, but I recommend doing it shortly after making your final payment. Once completed, the cruise line's system has all the required information about you and your traveling companions in advance, thereby saving a lot of time during check-in at the port. Once you are finished completing each of the online sections, you will print out a boarding pass (every cruise line calls it something different) and present it to the agent at the cruise port check-in desk along with your passport.

If you fail to complete your online check-in or lose your boarding pass, don't worry. Everything can be completed or replicated at the port. It's just a time-consuming process, and port authority security will have to manually look you up on the passenger manifest, no doubt with a few disapproving looks in the process! The only document the check-in desk can't replicate is your passport, without which you'll be refused boarding. Period. No exceptions.

One other advantage of online check-in is opening up the portal to make reservations and buy amenities for your cruise such as shore excursions, spa appointments, specialty dining, drink packages, and WiFi access. As I discussed earlier, some of these items – particularly shore excursions, sea day spa appointments, and the best specialty dining reservation times – may fill up before you even step on board. Each of these is covered in more detail in **Chapter 9**.

One important section of online check-in that may seem unnecessary is your flight itinerary, but the cruise line uses this information to determine when to schedule your final departure from the ship. If you have a relatively early flight on Debarkation Day, they'll put you in one of the first departure groups to ensure you get to the airport on time.

Otherwise, I suggest leaving the ship as late as possible to avoid the crowds, just as long as you can comfortably make your flight or other plans for the day.

If you're staying in the destination city for another day or two, you might be anxious to get off the ship and start exploring, but the ease of a later departure is worth it. Trust me.

Air Travel

One of the classic *faux pas* when it comes to flying to meet one's cruise is doing so on the day of sailing. Air travel delays happen all the time for a myriad of reasons, and if you don't make it to your departure port on time, the ship will leave without you. It's not like a land-based hotel that's not going anywhere if you're running late!

Therefore, I always recommend flying in the day before a cruise, or even a few days beforehand to enjoy the port city itself. If it's a locale not particularly worth exploring, then get there late on the day before sailing, have a relaxing evening at the hotel, order some room service, and leisurely head over to the cruise port the next day. Don't start your vacation at an unnecessarily high stress level or, God forbid, miss your ship entirely.

On Debarkation Day, I recommend leaving the ship as late as possible by scheduling an afternoon flight or staying another day or two to explore your final port of call. Most passengers are in a rush to get off the ship, resulting in bottlenecks, long lines and short tempers. Instead of getting caught up in all that insanity, let your fellow passengers rush off early while you depart at your leisure. Have a nice breakfast in the dining room and enjoy an extra cup of coffee or tea...or even a Bloody Mary. Why not?

TIP: If you're traveling internationally to meet your cruise, don't automatically book your flights at published fares. Ask your travel agent or cruise line about bulk or consolidated airfares, some of which are allocated specifically to cruise passengers. You may save a bundle.

Pre- and Post-Cruise Hotels

More often than not, I book my clients' pre- and post-cruise hotels away from the crowds. This usually allows them to avoid cruise passenger chaos in the lobby at check-out, and it frequently saves them money as well.

Granted, you won't be able to take the cruise line's pre-arranged transfer to the ship if you don't stay at their partner hotel, but I usually recommend against their transportation unless there's a significant distance between the hotel and the port.

See the next section on **Ground Transfers** for more details.

Ground Transfers

Most first-time cruisers opt for the cruise line's organized motorcoach transfers to and from the ship to ensure they get to the right place at the right time. It takes all the guesswork out of the equation, and there's nothing wrong with that.

However, cruise lines charge for transfers on a per-person basis. Thus, the larger your group, the more you'll save by taking a private car or taxi. Taxis are quick, cheap and easy, and you'll avoid being hauled around with the masses or waiting for your luggage to be unloaded from the underbelly of the bus.

The only exception to my "rule" is when there's a significant distance between the city where your hotel or airport is located and the cruise port. Three prime examples are London, Paris and Rome.

Even in these cases, I still recommend comparing the cost of the cruise-line motorcoach transfer to a privately booked vehicle and determining which one makes the most sense for you. Even if the private vehicle is slightly more, the comfort, ease and luxury may be worth the difference.

> **TIP:** The more people you have in your group, the less you'll pay per person for a private car, van or bus. Sometimes, even a chauffeured luxury sedan for two can be less than the cruise-line transfer, so it's worthwhile to do the research or ask your travel agent.

Packing

Packing for trips is a developed skill. If you've ever seen the movie *Up in the Air* with George Clooney, where he travels non-stop for a living, you may remember the scene where he roots through his new protégé's baggage, tossing "unnecessary items" in the trash and forcing her to buy a proper wheeled carry-on bag to avoid wasting time at baggage claim.

That was my life for quite some time, traveling on roughly 100 flights a year, and I can relate to the packing efficiencies one develops over time. Those practices make travel easier and less burdensome, eliminating the multiple heavy suitcases, paying exorbitant airline baggage fees for extra and/or overweight bags, chasing down luggage carts or porters at every turn, sorting through multiple bags to find your "stuff", and pulling muscles.

As it pertains to cruises, packing light is a splendid idea because storage in most cabins is limited, from hanging space in the closet to the number of available drawers and cabinets. That's why I recommend packing a limited number of color-coordinated wardrobe components that can be mixed and matched to create multiple outfits. This includes shoes, which can easily get out of hand. It's also smart to bring accessories, like a scarf or two, that can be used to change the appearance of a single outfit.

Admittedly, this is extra challenging since cruises typically require an assortment of clothing. You'll need swimwear for the pools and hot tubs, even in cold-weather climates since there's usually a pool area covered by a retractable roof. If you plan on using the fitness center, which is a great idea considering all the calories you'll consume, work-out attire is required. During the day, you'll need comfortable clothing such as shorts, jeans, short-sleeve shirts, T-shirts, sweats, etc. For dinner, a combination of casual, dressy casual, and formal attire is required, though some cruise lines stay dressy casual throughout the voyage. Be sure to check with the cruise line or your travel advisor for the dress code before you start the packing process. See **Dress Code** in **Chapter 12** for more specific details on daytime and evening wear.

Naturally, other than clothing, you should pack the same essentials you would include for any other trip including cosmetics, toiletries, hair implements, medications, first-aid supplies, etc. After that, it's a judgment call based on the locale and duration of your voyage. Note: almost all cruise ship staterooms include a hair dryer, and irons are prohibited, so leave those items at home.

The cruise line's online check-in section should have a link to a recommended pack list for your particular cruise, but here's a list of items people may forget. Some won't apply to you, and some will. It all depends on where you're going, your personal needs, and the quantity or types of clothing you plan to bring along:

- Sunscreen
- Moisturizer
- Hand sanitizer (stations will be all over the ship, too)
- Band-Aids (for blisters from all that walking)
- Tampons and pads
- Tote bag or small backpack for shore excursions
- Travel umbrella
- A light windbreaker (in case it unexpectedly rains)
- A light sweater (for cool nights on deck)
- Non-bulky hangers (for extra hanging clothes)
- Books and magazines (if you're old school)
- iPad/tablet/laptop and the corresponding **chargers**
- CPAP machines (must be with your carry-on luggage)
- Power adapters for your overseas pre- and post-hotels
- Your favorite camera or GoPro
- Binoculars
- Small inflatable water toys for kids
- Champagne corker for leftover bubbly in your cabin
- 3-Way adapters or extension cords for older ships
- Foldable duffle bag (to bring home gifts & souvenirs)
- Ziploc bags (for storing or protecting all sorts of things)
- Snack bars (for shore excursions and any travel delays)

If you are sailing on a longer cruise, such as 10 days or more, it might be tempting to pack extra clothes. But all cruise ships offer laundry services and sometimes even self-service laundromats, so dirty clothes won't become an issue.

Granted, there's usually no limit or charge for the number of suitcases you bring on board, but you may have trouble finding space for the contents, not to mention the bags themselves. You may be able to stow one or two empty suitcases under the bed(s), but the rest will probably clutter your room or crowd your wardrobe in the closet.

If you can't live without an extensive wardrobe and need multiple suitcases, try stacking smaller bags inside the larger ones before storing them to save space.

Finally, pack your valuables, medications and other essentials in your carry-on bag rather than in the suitcase(s) you check at the pier because the latter won't be delivered to your stateroom until late afternoon or evening on Embarkation Day.

If your plan is to hang out by the pool on Embarkation Day, be sure to pack a bathing suit, cover-up, sandals, and sunscreen in that carry-on bag to avoid being overdressed. All of the veteran cruisers around you will be well-prepared and decked out in their pool attire, so you should, too.

Things You Can't Bring on a Cruise Ship

There are two primary factors impacting what you can't bring on board a cruise ship – safety and cruise line profitability.

From a safety and security standpoint, cruise lines must prevent guests from having any implements that could be used to harm others (i.e., weapons) or items that run the risk of causing a fire or other hazardous incident, which could potentially injure the passengers or crew. This includes anything with a heating element or otherwise has flammable properties.

Items that impact the cruise line's profitability are essentially alcoholic beverages, which drive a significant portion of their sales. The reason other beverages are disallowed is because alcohol can be easily substituted, and security can't feasibly check the contents of every container.

Here's a list of commonly prohibited items, and it's a safe bet anything "similar" will be disallowed, too:

- Hard liquor and beer
- Wine and Champagne (except any allowed quantity)
- Non-alcoholic beverages including bottled water
- Clothing irons and steamers
- Heating pads
- Household appliances (coffee makers, hot plates, etc.)
- Candles and incense
- Hookahs
- Flammable or hazardous liquids like lighter fluid
- Guns
- Swords and knives with blades exceeding 4"
- Handcuffs
- Large items like bicycles, surfboards, kayaks and canoes
- Large coolers
- Inflatable pools

CPAP machines and the associated distilled water are allowed, but must be carried on board, not packed in checked bags.

Making a List (and checking it twice)

It may seem odd that a travel expert should have to tell anyone to make checklists when preparing for a trip, but I've seen far too many people plan and pack on the fly, only to show up at their destination without important documents, toiletries, medications, various clothing items, and other necessities. This is even worse for a cruise since replacing these items may be difficult, especially while on board the ship. The shops can only stock so much.

Besides, making a packing list helps you go through the mental exercise of planning outfits, deciding on the accessories you need, revealing what should be purchased before leaving home, whittling down a travel wardrobe that's just too large, and ensuring mission-critical items like your **passport** and cruise **boarding pass** get packed. Again, you will be refused boarding without a passport, so check one last time before you leave that it's in your purse, pocket, briefcase or carry-on bag. Yes, you may have proactively packed it two weeks ago, but what if you took it out to enter your passport details on the cruise line's website and forgot to put it back?

In addition to a packing list, I recommend making a **To-Do List**. There are so many things to be done before you leave town to prepare for the trip and hold down the fort while you're away. Here's a sample list of to-dos that may apply to you:

- Complete your online cruise and airline check-ins
- Print your cruise and airline boarding passes
- Print your cruise luggage tags (for checked bags)
- Print 2 copies of your third-party shore excursion vouchers
- Print or download your deck plans (see next section)
- Get travel cash including any foreign currency if you don't plan on using an ATM in your destination country(ies)
- Make copies of your passport, including a cell phone photo
- Give your itinerary to a friend or family member along with the ship's direct phone number in case of an emergency
- Make pet care arrangements or reservations
- Put your mail on hold
- Set up an out-of-office email message
- Inform your credit card issuer(s) of your travel plans
- Buy international and cruise ship calling and/or data plans from your cell carrier if you need them (most people don't)
- If you don't buy a data plan, turn OFF data roaming on your cell phone
- Tell your neighbors about your travel plans, and ask them to keep an eye on things while you're gone
- Check the weather shortly before you leave and plan a travel-day outfit that works at home and your destination
- Ask your travel agent for an airport parking discount coupon

Be sure to check your lists one more time before walking out the door. You never know when that underwear you thought you packed never made it into your suitcase because Aunt Agatha called to complain about her arthritis while you were rooting through your unmentionables, and it broke your packing mojo!

Studying Deck Plans

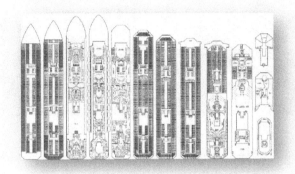

It's a great idea to study the deck plans of your ship in advance to get "the lay of the land" before you step on board. Granted, unless you have a photographic memory, you won't be able to memorize *everything*. But you can at least formulate a game plan for when you first step on board, not to mention figuring out where your stateroom is located relative to important venues like the main dining room, the pool, the nearest bar, etc.

All cruise line websites have sections highlighting their individual ships, and you can usually download the deck plans in PDF format. Sometimes it's necessary to do it deck-by-deck, but a few lines allow a one-time download of the entire ship. There are also third-party websites with downloadable deck plans, but they may not always be accurate or current. Cruise ships frequently undergo alterations, if not a full-fledged dry dock refurbishment, so any deck plans you obtain will be accurate for a particular period of time. Make sure they correspond with your travel dates.

Of course, you can always ask your travel agent to send them to you, as he or she has access to cruise line resources you don't, including full sets of PDF deck plans.

Regardless of how you obtain them, I suggest printing off the full set of deck plans or downloading the PDF version to your tablet, phone or laptop. You'll be free to review them during your outbound flight(s) or at the hotel the night before you sail. You can also consult them throughout the cruise and carry them with you as you roam the ship.

> **TIP:** The cruise line will probably hand you a set of foldable deck plans when you check in at the pier, or you can pick up a copy at the Passenger Services desk, but these are often small and difficult to read, especially for people who routinely use reading glasses. Having a larger printed set or zoomable plans on a mobile device can be extra helpful.

CHAPTER 11: EMBARKATION DAY

Arriving at the Cruise Port

Most likely, your initial departure port will be a large facility with several cruise ships docked at various piers. There may also be multiple terminals, possibly located some  distance from each other. Therefore, it's important to make sure you're going to the right place. A great example of this is the bustling cruise port in Barcelona, Spain, pictured above.

If you've arranged for professional private transportation or booked the cruise line's designated motorcoach, you'll be fine. If you're taking a taxi or driving your own car (to be parked at the cruise terminal), it's important to know the exact pier where your ship is berthed. Fortunately, most cruise ports provide digital message boards after you enter the facility to direct you to the correct pier, but it's always a good idea to consult with the cruise line a week or two before your sailing date to get the exact location for yourself. Better yet, call your travel agent.

Most cruise ships begin the boarding process around 11:00 or Noon, no matter what time the ship is scheduled to leave the port. It can happen as late as 1:00, but usually no later than that. It's impossible to know for sure because the ship will have offloaded most (if not all) of its previous passengers throughout the morning hours, and it takes time for the cruise line, immigration, and the port authority to clear the ship for re-boarding. Passengers who have arrived and checked in must remain in the port building's waiting area until that happens.

On the other side of the equation, cruise lines have strict policies regarding how *late* a passenger may board, and it's usually 60 to 90 minutes in advance of scheduled departure. This is for a number of reasons, one of which is to leave enough time before sailing to conduct the passenger muster drill in accordance with maritime law. See **The Mandatory Muster Drill** later in this section.

In addition, port authorities enforce various lead times for the ship's crew to deliver a final passenger manifest in advance of sailing. That means you can't rely on the cruise line's policy by default. Instead, obtain the exact check-in schedule for your particular sailing (something like 11:00am to 3:00pm) and make sure you arrive before the window closes. This can usually be found on the boarding pass you printed off from the cruise line's website. Otherwise, check with the cruise line directly or give your travel agent a call. If you arrive after the deadline, the port authority probably won't allow you to board, even if the ship remains there with the gangway attached for another hour or so.

Depending on the cruise line, you may be assigned a more specific check-in window to avoid crowding at the port, and it will be printed on your cruise boarding pass. If you arrive beforehand, they will make you wait. Arriving late, but still within the overall check-in schedule, won't be an issue. Cruise lines are aware that travelers can be affected by a myriad of travel delays.

If passengers aren't assigned a check-in window, most of them will arrive as early as possible to "get the party started", especially if they've purchased an unlimited drink package. Therefore, the port building will be more congested during the first hour or so of the check-in process. If you're one of those people who isn't fond of crowds, I recommend arriving 1½ to 2 hours after the check-in process begins.

Once you arrive at the port, the first order of business will be to hand over you checked luggage. The porters should be near your drop-off point, and cruise line representatives will be there to direct you as well. We'll cover this in more detail shortly.

Port Parking

If you drive to meet your cruise and plan to park at the port, I recommend researching the parking facilities in advance. In most cases, particularly in the US, the cruise port will have its own parking lots or even a garage facility, much like an airport.

As an alternative, there are usually third-party parking facilities nearby with shuttles regularly running back and forth while ships are in port. Like third-party lots near airports, the parking charges will be somewhat less.

Checked Versus Carry-On Luggage

There is no charge to check luggage at the pier and have it delivered to your stateroom, so don't lug your larger bags all the way through security and up the potentially steep ramps to the ship. Besides, most cruise lines limit the size of carry-on bags to whatever will fit through the X-Ray machines at security. In general, carry-on luggage should not exceed 16 inches in height or 24 inches in width (41cm x 61cm). Length is usually not a factor.

Checked luggage must be properly tagged before you hand it to the porters at the pier, and you should customarily tip them a dollar or two per bag (or Euro, Pound, etc.). I recommend tagging your checked luggage before you leave the hotel or airport, thereby eliminating frustration at the bustling cruise port facility. If you've lost your luggage tags, the porter can prepare new ones for you, but tip them a little extra. It's also a good idea to tag your carry-on bags in case they are lost or left unattended on the ship as you wait for your stateroom to become available.

Baggage tags can usually be printed in whatever quantity you need from the online check-in section of the cruise line's website on letter-sized paper, preferably in color. You will fold and staple that sheet over the primary handle on your bag. The easy folding instructions are printed on the paper itself. If you are staying in a hotel the night before your cruise (which I recommend), you can borrow a stapler from the front desk, as hotels in port areas are accustomed to that request.

However, I always pack a tiny travel stapler to attach the tags before leaving the hotel room, and it's extra handy if you need to tag luggage at the airport after retrieving it from baggage claim (assuming you flew in the same day of your cruise and are taking transportation directly to the cruise port).

Again, I usually recommend against flying in on the day of a cruise, as you run the risk of flight delays or cancellations causing you to miss the ship. However, if you're flying between two major US airports very early in the morning, with multiple later flights that would successfully get you there on time should you have a flight cancellation, I suppose I can look the other way. Just expect to hear a heavy sigh of disapproval on my end!

Okay, back to your luggage. Your larger bags will be safely checked in with the porters, and you'll retain at least one carry-on bag with your valuables, medications, travel documents and anything else you need until roughly 6:00pm on Embarkation Day, as it may take that long before your checked luggage arrives at your stateroom. If you plan to hang by the pool, you should pack a bathing suit, cover-up, sunblock and sandals in your carry-on bag.

Once your larger suitcases do arrive, they will be placed in the hallway outside your cabin because the porters do not have room keys. If you've booked a suite with a butler, he will most likely bring the bags inside and, if instructed to do so, unpack them for you.

Outside Wine/Alcohol

Some cruise lines will allow you to carry on two 750ML bottles of wine or Champagne per stateroom when you board the ship on Embarkation Day. Others will not, so check your cruise line's policies before attempting to do so. Any other alcohol from beer to distilled spirits are never allowed, and most lines now prohibit all other bottled beverages, including water. After all, water looks a lot like Vodka, and they can't test every single bottle.

Fortunately, most lines will log and tag any disallowed alcohol when they take it away and arrange to return it to you at the end of the cruise. The ship makes a good portion of its income by selling alcoholic beverages, so they are already being generous with the wine allowance.

If you do bring the allowed wine or Champagne on board, DO NOT pack it in your checked luggage. Put it in your carry-on bag or carry it separately during the check-in process so you can properly claim it. Otherwise, it will be found in your checked luggage and confiscated, never to be seen again. Checked and carry-on bags are thoroughly scanned for alcohol and items the cruise line deems to be dangerous such as candles, irons and weapons.

If you attempt to bring alcohol or additional wine on board at *any other* port during the cruise, it will be treated the same way as disallowed alcohol at the original port of call – logged and returned to you at the end of the cruise. The only difference is that security won't scoff at you for violating the rules. They are aware that wines and spirits are common purchases at ports of call to be taken home.

I've heard claims that a passenger can fool the system by carrying a glass flask of spirits through security in their pocket because there will be no metal to set off the "metal" detector. But those detectors (both the archway and handheld versions) sense liquids as well as metal, and the flask will be taken away.

> **TIP:** Do away with all the stress by purchasing an unlimited alcohol package and let loose for the duration of your cruise. I can assure you that no one will spontaneously ask you to be the designated driver of the ship!

Port Authority Screening and Security

No matter where you first board a cruise ship, whether it's in the US or abroad, the applicable port authority will conduct a two-stage screening and security process before you are cleared to proceed to the check-in desks. Some ports outside the US may conduct the security screening *after* check-in, but that's not common.

The first stage is an examination of your cruise documents, passport, any visas required for the ports of call, and a statement of health, although the statement of health is more frequently being filled out at the cruise line check-in desk.

The statement of health is a one-page questionnaire that will be provided to you somewhere inside the port building, and you may encounter people scrambling for pens and filling out the forms on any surface they can find, including each other's backs, often while proceeding through line. That's because few port buildings provide adequate surface area for everyone to use.

The second stage is a physical security screening similar to a TSA checkpoint at an airport, although you won't have to deal with one of those full-body scanners, and liquids in excess of 3 ounces won't be taken away (except for beverages). If you are bringing aboard the wine or Champagne that MAY be allowed by your cruise line (see the earlier section on **Outside Wine/Alcohol**), this is where you should claim it.

It usually isn't necessary to take laptops or other electronics out of carry-on bags, or to remove shoes, but people are asked to take off heavier coats.

The port authority metal detectors are usually very sensitive, probably to aid in liquid detection, so you should remove cell phones, other electronics, and metal objects from your pockets. Larger belt-buckles are likely to set off the detector, too, but I'll leave it to you whether to take them off in advance or risk having to remove them before your second run. If you set it off a second time, an official will take you aside to be scanned with a wand, but the process rarely ever reaches the level of invasiveness of a private TSA secondary screening.

Throughout the trip, you will be required to pass through a metal detector and have a baggage X-Ray check as you re-board the ship at each port of call, but it is a more simplified process, and the only documentation you'll need is your cruise card. However, the port authority at any stop may also conduct its own security and immigration screening before you reach the ship, so it's a good idea to carry your passport on shore. See **What You Should Take with You** in **Chapter 13**.

TIP: Bring pens for everyone in your group. It will speed up filling out your health questionnaires and avoid having to borrow from others. Even better, buy some cheap pens and leave them behind for your fellow passengers. It's a random act of kindness that will be sincerely appreciated.

Checking In

After security, you will come across a sea of check-in desks, and each cruise line organizes them differently. However, there will usually be a VIP section for suite passengers and the elite members of the cruise line's  loyalty program, much like the first class/priority check-in counters for airlines. They may also have separate desks for passengers booked in other types of premium staterooms such as Concierge Class and Aqua Class on Celebrity. Everyone else uses the standard check-in area, which will have a lengthy line the first hour or so unless passengers are assigned check-in windows.

It's easier if passengers who are booked in the same stateroom check in at the same time, though not essential since cabin mates may not be traveling together to the port. It's also helpful if families check in together, even if they're staying in multiple cabins. If one of those family members is booked in a suite, the cruise line will usually allow the rest of the family to join them at the suite VIP check-in. However, the likelihood of this special treatment decreases in direct proportion to the size of your group. If your family has 10 cabins, don't count on it.

At the desk, you will once again hand over your cruise boarding pass, passport, and visas (if applicable). If you entered all of your information online in advance, including the credit card to be used for your onboard account, the agent will scan that credit card into the system, provide you with your cruise card(s), and send you on your way. If your record is missing any information, the agent will obtain it from you and enter everything in the computer while you wait.

It is also possible to pay for a cruise with cash, whereby the passenger settles his or her bill at the Passenger Services Desk the last night of the cruise. Each cruise line's policy is different on this, so be sure to check in advance what is required, such as an advance cash deposit.

If you arrive at the embarkation port and discover that you've lost your cruise documents, it's not the end of the world. They can be recreated at the check-in desk. It just prolongs the process, and you may have an awkward moment with port security as they look you up on the passenger manifest, especially if you're in a foreign country and don't speak the language.

If you lose your passport (or other required ID), you won't be allowed to board. If you don't have the visas required for your trip (if any), you won't be allowed to board.

Someone along the way will take an "official" photo of you, and this is typically done at the check-in desk, but sometimes at a special kiosk on your way to the ship. The photo will show up on a screen each time your cruise card is scanned as you board or depart the ship, thereby allowing security personnel to confirm who you are. Be sure you don't accidentally grab your cabin mate's cruise card because they'll detain you if the picture doesn't match.

TIP: Sometimes the regular check-in counters will be segregated by the first letter of the passenger's last name. If that's the case, and the passengers in your stateroom have different last names, use whichever line is shorter.

Your Cruise Card and Onboard Account

Your cruise card, provided to you during the check-in process, is similar in appearance to a hotel key card including the magnetic strip on the back. It provides access to your stateroom, serves as your ID to get on and off the ship, and acts

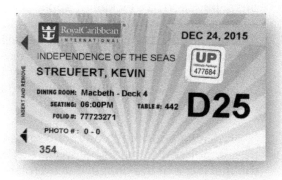

as your charge card everywhere on board. It sometimes even works for purchases on the cruise line's private island if you're going there. Cruises are cashless, so you can leave your wallet or purse in the stateroom safe while you're galivanting around the ship.

Everything charged to your cruise card is added to your onboard account. At the end of the cruise, the balance of your cruise account will be charged to your credit card (if you have so authorized), or you will be required to settle the account in cash with the Passenger Services Desk prior to debarkation.

A printout of your account reflecting the outstanding balance and a detail of every charge during the voyage will be delivered to your cabin the final night of the cruise. This will give you a chance to review the transactions and discuss any discrepancies with the Passenger Services Desk or your concierge, if applicable, prior to your credit card being charged or otherwise settling the account.

Each passenger in a stateroom may have his/her own onboard account, or everyone can be set up on the same account. During the online check-in process, you will set up your onboard account and optionally authorize one or more passengers from the same cabin or any other cabin to charge to it. This is usually how onboard accounts for spouses and families are set up, whereby the charges from each member's cruise card are combined. The printout delivered on the final night will break out the transactions by cruise card, allowing the primary passenger (i.e., the responsible party) to determine who made each charge.

Boarding

Once the cruise line, immigration and port authority have cleared the ship for boarding, passengers who are checked in and waiting in the cruise terminal lounge will board in groups, with suite guests and premium loyalty members going first. Once the backlog has been eliminated, anyone else arriving at the port will board immediately after checking in.

On your way to the ship, you will likely follow a maze through the port building, possibly with escalators or stairs, ultimately leading you to a gangway connected to the ship. These ramps can be steep, so those with mobility issues or who are out of shape should consider requesting a wheelchair. Otherwise, they can just take their time and let others pass by.

Somewhere along the way, you are likely to come across one or more photographers taking pictures of people in front of a large poster of the ship. This will be the first of many photo ops during your cruise vacation, and they are all optional. Feel free to say, "no thanks," and continue on your way. But, there's no charge for these photos unless you buy them later, so why not? See **Professional Photo Opportunities** in **Chapter 12** for more information.

Depending on what time you make it on board, the staterooms may not be ready for occupancy. Most people head to a bar, restaurant or pool area to grab a seat, eat some lunch, and perhaps grab a cocktail or two.

At some point, an announcement will be made that the staterooms are ready, usually around 2:00, but there's no reason why you can't start having fun in the meantime. I suggest combing through the deck plans of the ship in advance and map out a strategy for when you arrive on board.

Embarkation Day Lunch and Libations

After the sometimes-arduous process of getting to the port and going through check-in and boarding, most people are starving and ready for lunch. The main dining room and specialty restaurants will likely be closed, but there should be plenty of other options.

The most popular venue will be the ship's buffet restaurant, usually located near the top of the ship, often on the same deck as the main pool. See **The Buffet Restaurant** in **Chapter 5** for more details.

Another option will be the grill counter near the pool, serving burgers, dogs, sausages, brats, fries and maybe even onion rings. This is all you can eat, remember? So, don't be shy. There may not be a poolside grill counter if the cruise line has a specialty burger restaurant, but you'll have plenty of other options. Or, you can scope out the location of the specialty burger place in advance and keep your fingers crossed that it's open on Embarkation Day.

If you're a pizza lover, there will be an outlet somewhere on the ship with endless slices ready to go. It may be on the pool deck or down on the Promenade. Again, do some research in advance to ensure you don't miss out.

If you ate a huge lunch before heading to the port and just want a snack to hold you until dinner, try the specialty coffee bar. Most likely, they'll have small croissant sandwiches as well as other choice snacks and sweets to fit the bill.

When it comes to alcoholic drinks, pretty much every bar will be open, and the bartenders will happily serve you anything you want, again and again, whether you're purchasing à la carte or using an unlimited drink package.

You can order a burger at the grill, grab the beer of your choice next door at the bar while you wait, and you're set. Or, bask by the pool and drink the tropical cocktail of the day, as one after another is delivered to you by a charming waiter. Or, use your culinary savvy to create a perfect meal at the buffet restaurant, then pair it with the perfect glass of wine from the adjacent bar. The Embarkation Day game plans are virtually limitless.

Accessing Your Stateroom

Once the staterooms are ready for occupancy, everyone will get situated in their cabins. Shortly thereafter, they'll put whatever they're doing on hold while they participate in The Mandatory Muster Drill (see the next section).

As noted earlier, your luggage may take until 6:00 or later to reach your stateroom. Thus, it is important to pack everything you need for Embarkation Day in your carry-on bag. If you signed up for the early seating at dinner, rest assured that the dress code will be casual for the first night, and whatever you wore during the boarding process is probably acceptable in the main dining room. Just don't wear your bikini, cover-up and sandals. If that's your choice of eveningwear, eat at the buffet restaurant instead.

The Mandatory Muster Drill

What in the world is a "muster drill", you may ask? It's an exercise to instruct you how to proceed in the event your ship goes the way of the *Titanic* or *Lusitania*. This is also referred to as the "life boat drill". In the unlikely event the ship comes in imminent danger of sinking, you'll know what to do.

Granted, with today's state-of-the-art ships and technology, such an incident is extremely rare, but maritime law requires the ship to conduct a drill with each set of new passengers to ensure they are familiar with emergency procedures. Think of it like the safety briefing before a commercial flight... on steroids.

Putting the seriousness of this important safety protocol aside, many veteran cruisers affectionately refer to this exercise as the "mustard drill", which brings about images of people sporting mustard squeeze bottles, dousing each other in a frenzied melee. But, I digress.

Each cruise line conducts their muster drills in a different manner. The traditional way is for all passengers to gather at their assigned muster station on the life boat deck (usually the Promenade Deck) carrying a life vest from their stateroom. They are subsequently instructed how to put on and secure the life vest, practicing the procedure while listening to the narrated instructions over the PA system and observing their muster station leader.

The problem with this traditional practice is that many people allow the life vest straps to drag behind them, especially up and down the stairways (elevators are shut down during the drill), and there have been incidents of tripping over the years, sometimes resulting in injuries.

Therefore, most cruise lines have transitioned to doing their muster drills in various alternate venues on the ship, such as the main theater, lounges and dining rooms. People no longer bring their life vests, but simply observe crew members demonstrating the procedure. The passengers in each muster station are assigned to a designated area within each venue. In an actual emergency, that's exactly where they will meet before being systematically routed to their muster stations to board the life boats.

The muster drill is mandatory for all passengers, and roll is called for each station. If you fail to attend, the ship is required by maritime law to make you do a make-up drill or escort you off the ship at their earliest opportunity. All restaurants, bars and lounges are closed for the duration, thereby helping to ensure everyone's participation.

Most people have had a cocktail or two by the time the muster drill happens, so it is usually marked by joviality and smiles. In other words, you should consider it part of the "fun" of your cruise vacation.

CHAPTER 12: LIFE ON BOARD

Daily Program

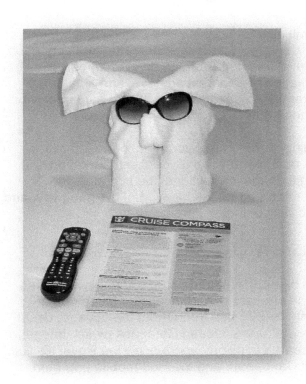

All cruise lines deliver a daily program to your stateroom every evening with a schedule of events and activities for the next day. It also includes port information (if applicable), special onboard deals, weather, tips, shipboard procedures, and other important postings. On Embarkation Day, a program will be waiting in your stateroom to help plan your first afternoon and evening on board.

These newsletters often have cute or clever names like *The Princess Patter* on Princess Cruise Lines, *Cruise Compass* on Royal Caribbean (shown above), and *Fun Times* on Carnival. They're a great tool to help plan your time, especially during sea days and evenings.

Most people check out the various performances and passenger participation events each evening and formulate a plan around dinner. Each show in the main theater is usually offered twice, timed against the early and late dinner seatings to ensure everyone has an opportunity to see it. Events elsewhere on the ship may occur just once, and it can sometimes be a challenge to work in the ones you'd like to attend, especially around dinner. In cases like this, it sometimes makes sense to hit a specialty restaurant or the buffet at an earlier or later time.

The newsletter will also list opening and closing times for restaurants and other venues across the ship. They will vary each day based on the arrival and departure times at each port of call, the impact of embarkation or debarkation days, and a myriad of other factors. For example, breakfast hours will be earlier for a port arrival at 7:00am than at 8:00am.

On the last evening of the cruise, your final newsletter (or a completely separate document) will provide disembarkation information including luggage instructions, the schedule for staggered passenger departures, the location of the gangway, and settling your onboard account.

Cruise Line Onboard App

One of the latest high-tech features cruise lines have started adding to enhance the onboard experience is a mobile app or browser-accessed interface to use throughout the voyage. Great examples are Princess Cruises' Ocean Compass (which integrates with its ship-wide Ocean Medallion experience), the Royal IQ mobile app on Royal Caribbean, and the Hub mobile app from Carnival.

Each uses the ship's WiFi network without requiring a WiFi package, which you would only purchase for full-fledged Internet access, if you so desire. With or without Internet access, these systems allow people to perform multiple tasks such as messaging with your fellow passengers (sometimes for a small fee), viewing the day's activities & entertainment, ordering food & drinks, browsing restaurant menus, making dinner reservations, reading port guides, booking shore excursions, keeping track of your shipboard account, viewing your itinerary, exploring the ship's deck plans, getting directions to onboard venues, shopping for shipboard merchandise, accessing weather forecasts, and even playing games.

The idea is not only to modernize and streamline your cruise experience, but allow the crew to serve you more intuitively by acting on information collected throughout the voyage. Should you have privacy concerns, you can easily opt out of the program and cruise the old-fashioned way.

Stateroom Television

Chances are, you won't be watching a lot of TV during your cruise vacation, except when you're taking a break to relax in your stateroom between climbing the rock wall and heading to the pool. But the television in your cabin is more than just a source of entertainment.

First, you can usually find information on tomorrow's port of call, including details about the port facility itself. It should inform you whether the ship will be docked or anchored (in which case you'll take a tender to the shore), any immigration procedures, required documentation to take with you, dos and don'ts, etc. There should also be plenty of information about the city and its surrounding area, important sites, and perhaps some interesting historical or cultural facts. If you're really lucky, they will replay an enrichment lecture given on the ship by a local expert or historian.

On the last full day of your cruise, a channel will be dedicated to the final debarkation process, which can be confusing for first-time cruisers. It can even throw off people who have sailed before, as procedures are different from one cruise line to the next, and they are always subject to change, presumably for the better. This program will be repeated over and over, just in case you miss something important the first time around. Or the second!

On the lighter side, some of the television programming can be fun, which might come in handy if you're exhausted or not feeling well, prompting you to spend a little time in bed. On Princess ships, one channel is dedicated entirely to *Love Boat* reruns, which will give you a great appreciation for how far the cruise industry has come since the 1970s and 80s!

Announcements

During the day, announcements will be made throughout the ship to spread timely or important information such as muster drill instructions, the readiness of staterooms on Embarkation Day, the ship's clearance for debarkation at a new port, the location of the gangway (such as "Deck 4, Midship"), the commencement of an "exciting" onboard event, etc.

Matters considered to be critical, like instructions for the muster drill or announcing a last-minute itinerary change, will be piped through the speaker in your stateroom. All other announcements, such as arrival and clearance updates at a scheduled port of call, will only be broadcast in the hallways and other common areas of the ship. The idea is not to disturb people with information they may not care about.

As non-critical announcements begin, people will often scramble to their stateroom doors and crack them open to hear the information, especially if they're planning to get off the ship and hope to find out where the gangway is located. If you're walking down the passageway and catch a glimpse, try not to judge their choice of pajamas…or boxer shorts.

Debarkation instructions on the last day of the cruise will also be piped into your stateroom. Announcements will occur throughout the morning as each departure group is cleared to leave the ship, even after the deadline for passengers to vacate their staterooms. See **Chapter 14** for more details.

Your Cabin Steward

Your cabin steward provides so much more than maid service for your stateroom. He or she is charged with a long list of responsibilities to ensure your onboard life and accommodations are as comfortable as possible.

The first order of business, before you even arrive, is to arrange your beds in the configuration you or your travel agent identified in advance. If they somehow aren't correct, just let the steward know when you first meet, and he or she will reconfigure them before bedtime, usually while you're at dinner.

Each evening, your steward will perform turn-down service in your stateroom, which not only entails preparing the bed, but also doing a light cleaning, emptying trash, replacing towels, etc. If you have 3 or more guests in your room, your steward will pull out the additional beds (whether it's the couch or an upper berth that folds out of the ceiling or wall) and make them up accordingly.

In the morning, once you've left the room to have breakfast or head on shore, your steward will return the extra beds to their concealed locations, thereby providing as much space as possible during waking hours.

Your steward will also make sure your laundry orders are delivered to housekeeping and hang your clothes back in the

closet upon their return. He or she will deliver your daily newsletter and any other important communications throughout the day, arrange for the repair of anything in the cabin that may not be working properly, and even make towel animals to surprise you upon your return most evenings.

I always enthusiastically introduce myself to the cabin steward on Embarkation Day, establish a friendly rapport, and insist he or she calls us by our first names. This makes the relationship more enjoyable throughout the cruise and encourages the steward to go above and beyond for us. If that happens, I'll slip him or her an appropriate amount of extra cash at the end of the cruise, in addition to the automatic daily gratuity charge.

Room Service

Many cruise lines offer room service at no charge (food only), and it can be a convenient way to have breakfast on early port days. However, unless you're traveling on a luxury cruise line like Crystal, Seabourn or Regent Seven Seas, expect the hot items in your order (like eggs) to be a tad on the cold side. It's a long way from the galley to your stateroom, and room service is likely handling hundreds of orders at the same time. Also, your food will probably be on a cart with a half dozen others headed for nearby staterooms, and it takes time to distribute everything. I encourage everyone to keep all this in mind before complaining. For a hot, delicious sit-down breakfast, head to the main dining room.

You'll also call Room Service to order bottled water, wine, beer, spirits and mixers for your stateroom. If you aren't there when the order arrives, your steward will arrange to have it placed inside. However, if you have an unlimited drink package, DO NOT order these items from Room Service because they won't be covered under your plan. Instead, go to the nearest bar, lounge, specialty coffee venue, etc.

If you're a suite guest with a butler, you'll give your room service orders to him, and he'll probably serve the food to you. On some higher-end lines, butlers will serve course-by-course meals in the stateroom or out on the veranda, often with your choice of food from any or all of the onboard restaurants.

Dining

I covered dining venues in **Chapter 5** and noted that people's evenings on a cruise are typically organized around dinner.

This is particularly true if your cruise includes formal or dressy nights, when getting ready for dinner takes on a whole new meaning. These nights also bring opportunities for professional photos in one or more areas of the ship, usually with tasteful backdrops. Budget extra time to wait in line if you wish to participate.

If you are too cool to dress up or don't want to go through the trouble, these nights are a good time to eat dinner at the buffet restaurant, the burger joint, the pizza place, or one of the other informal food outlets on the ship. The dining rooms and specialty restaurants are reserved for those conforming to the evening's guidelines. See **Dress Code** later in this section.

Entertainment and Activities

If you're a first-time cruiser and concerned about being bored, don't worry. Cruise ships offer entertainment and activities across such a broad spectrum that it's virtually impossible to be bored. If that happens, you're not looking hard enough.

We've already talked about the various entertainment venues around the ship and some of the shows or contests you can expect to see there (or participate in), but here are a few more events you might encounter, though it's far from comprehensive:

Performances	**Guest Participation**
Broadway-Type Shows	Wine Tastings
Stand-Up Comedy	Gambling Tournaments
Solo Musicians	Game Shows
Jazz Trios or Quartets	Trivia Contests
Classical Ensembles	Scavenger Hunts
Rock or Dance Bands	Karaoke
Cover Bands	Dancing
Dance Shows	Group Line Dancing
Magic Shows	Ballroom Lessons
Acrobatic Shows	Bridge Tournaments
Cooking Demonstrations	Cooking Classes
Enrichment Lectures	Ping Pong Tournaments

Art Auctions

It may seem odd to buy a piece of art on a cruise ship, particularly if it's a serious piece, but ever since art auctions on cruise ships started a couple of decades ago, they have turned into a serious business.

Auctions with free Champagne (and sometimes even free art) are conducted throughout a cruise, particularly on sea days, with the times and locations identified in your daily program. Usually, there are announcements over the ship's PA system shortly before each auction.

The art consists almost entirely of paintings, which are to be tagged by interested parties during the preview segment. These items will be brought up front by the gallery representative to auction off. Each piece of art will have a reserve amount, and if there's no bidding at that level, it will be returned to the viewing area. These works of art are usually available for browsing somewhere on the ship throughout the cruise, and you will recognize works by some of the more famous artists, like those whimsical olive paintings and burning $100 bills by Michael Goddard, or the wildly colorful works by Peter Max.

If you are the successful bidder, the gallery representative will meet with you after the auction to obtain your personal information and payment. A few weeks later, the piece will arrive at your home in a crate or other proper packaging, usually in a brand-new frame. If it is a signed and numbered work, you may not receive the exact piece you viewed on board, but another one from their land-based warehouse reflecting a different number in the series.

Most art auctions at sea are operated by Park West Gallery out of Southfield, Michigan – a reputable gallery that has been in business since 1969. Park West deals in great part with serious collectors and sells investment-grade art, including pieces from some of the foremost artists in recent history. In other words, I wouldn't worry about the authenticity of the works being offered on board the ship. Furthermore, it makes sense that any gallery authorized by a large cruise line should be equally trustworthy, but I can only attest to Park West from personal experience.

Rather than authenticity, the real question is price. If you're dealing with a fun piece in the hundreds of dollars that you'd love to hang on your wall, just bid until you win, and don't worry about the cost. On the other hand, if it's a serious work that will run thousands or more, it makes sense to inquire about the item's reserve price in advance and use the ship's WiFi to do some research. If it's a good deal, then great. If not, you might consider sharing your findings with the art gallery representative and see if the price can be lowered.

Very few of the higher-priced pieces in the ship's inventory will sell on any given cruise. Therefore, it's reasonable to assume you won't have any competition if you tag one for the auction, and the reserve price is what you'll pay. You can go through the entertainment of having the piece brought up front and win it as the sole bidder, no doubt eliciting applause and congratulatory handshakes from your fellow passengers. Or, you may be able to convince the gallery representative to sell it to you directly at the reserve price, which is much easier to do on the final day of the cruise, after the last auction has concluded.

Professional Photo Opportunities

Throughout your cruise, you will come across professional photographers asking to take your picture. This starts inside the port building before you even board the ship. They are also notorious for showing up at your dinner table as well as outside the ship after your shore excursions. Feel free to say no, especially if you're tired and worn out after a long day. But you might consider saying yes on formal nights when they set up elaborate stations around the ship for professional portraits.

Hard or digital copies of your photos will show up the next day in the photo gallery. Digital copies are easily accessed with a swipe of your cruise card, whereas hard copies are placed on racks and organized by the venue or day they were taken. Then it's a matter of scanning through the hundreds or thousands of photos to find your own. If you like how they turned out, you have the option of buying them, and copies can be made in whatever sizes or quantities you may desire.

If you've been thinking about having a professional portrait taken with your family, spouse, girlfriend or boyfriend, the well-crafted photos taken on formal or dressy nights may suit the bill. The quality is usually very good, and the photos will cost substantially less than going to a photo studio, so it doesn't hurt to wait in line and let the photographers snap a few shots. If the pictures don't turn out to your satisfaction, you don't have to buy them. It's a no-risk scenario.

Booking a Future Cruise

As if there weren't enough to keep you occupied on a cruise ship, you'll always have the option of booking your next cruise at the Future Cruise Desk.

The deals offered here are rarely cruise fare discounts. They typically consist of onboard credits and/or reduced deposits that aren't part of a promotion currently available to the public. In other words, you can book a new cruise under any existing fare deal PLUS get the incentives being offered on board. You might also get an onboard credit for the cruise you're taking right now.

What if you'd like to sail with this cruise line again, but have no idea when you'll be able to fit it in your schedule? Do an "open booking" that has no specified cruise itinerary or date, allowing you to select the cruise at some point in the future. That way, you grab the additional incentives without having to make a commitment right away.

There are two possible caveats. First, open bookings sometimes have an expiration date, like 12 or 24 months down the road. Second, reduced deposits are sometimes non-refundable, so be sure to ask the booking agent about both. If either poses a problem for you, it may not be worth doing. Unless, of course, your onboard credit for the current cruise is equal to the deposit for the *future* cruise, in which case you have nothing at risk.

If you do book a future cruise, rest assured that it doesn't cut your travel agent out of the deal. The cruise line recognizes you as their client and will notify them immediately of the new booking under the assumption they will take it the rest of the way.

Child Care/Activities

With a few exceptions, all cruise ships offer child care, and some lines elevate that concept to serious entertainment and enrichment programs with colorful spaces, lots of organized activities, and even visits from life-size cartoon characters. Clearly, a Disney cruise will be more child-focused than a Seabourn sailing, but there are other cruise lines with great youth programs as well.

Children are typically separated into as many as five age categories with appropriate activities for each. Simple nursery services, whether in your stateroom or the nursery itself, usually entail a minimum age of one year, though some activities may be designed for babies as young as six-months old with a parent in attendance.

Youth activities often include sensory play classes, games, arts & crafts, storytelling, putting on plays, treasure hunts, video games, low-impact sports, messy play, and even circus school.

Areas for children are safe and strictly controlled, with only parents authorized to enter the space or pick up their kids. The only exception is someone who the parents have specifically authorized to act on their behalf, like an adult child or nanny.

Teen Programs

Teens are usually free to come and go throughout the day, utilizing their space for entertainment and socializing with their peers.

Teen programs may include theme parties, dancing, karaoke, video game tournaments, sporting events, special dinners, movies, and team-building exercises. On occasion, these organized activities may move to other parts of the ship like the sport court, rock walls or other entertainment venues.

Families and Groups

Cruises have become an excellent venue for family and group vacations, in part because today's megaships are like floating cities with something for everyone. They're also a fun and exciting environment for the entire group to socialize, play together, eat together, and drink together. Then, at the end of the night, everyone makes it safely back "home", even those who might have partied a little too hard. You can't say that about a group trip to Vegas!

Groups warrant special attention on a cruise, and it's important to make plans as far in advance as possible. For example, reservations for everyone in a group should be linked together with identical dining times and table preferences so the maître d' in the main dining room can make arrangements to seat everyone together, or at least at adjacent tables. When I handle groups, I make sure all of that happens, and I ask detailed questions along the way to ensure the dining arrangements are exactly the way my clients want them.

However, let's not forget that cruise ship maître d's are very busy, and there's always a human element in the communication process. Therefore, I recommend that the point-person for each group touches base with the maître d' shortly after boarding to ensure everything is in order. That's far better than the whole group showing up at the dining room promptly at 6:00 (or 8:15 if you choose the late seating) with table assignments scattered all over the dining room. By then, it's too late to move things around.

Groups of a certain size may also reserve a selection of venues on board for private meetings, social gatherings, cocktail parties and such. Sometimes, if the participants are expected to order alcoholic drinks, the venue and snacks are provided at no charge, but there may still be a fee for each bartender and waitperson in attendance.

Finally, groups of 8 staterooms or more may qualify for special perks and pricing. The more you add, the better the deal. Ask your travel agent for details.

Laundry

All cruise ships offer laundry services from the housekeeping department, but they vary on cost and processes. Many of them function like the laundry service at a hotel, where you place your clothing in a bag, mark a ticket with the items enclosed, and they will charge you accordingly for each.

Some Mass Market cruise lines have started providing fabric laundry bags (also or instead) that you can stuff as full as possible, and the flat rate for cleaning everything is just $20 to $25, no matter how many items you manage to get in there. This is for regular laundry and does not include dry cleaning.

Some cruise ships also have self-service laundromats. If you are taking a longer cruise and plan to wash clothes once or twice along the way, check to see if your ship has one, but if they offer the flat-rate laundry bag option, it hardly seems worth your time.

Dress Codes

Dress
codes vary
from one
cruise line to
the next,
sometimes
quite a bit.
Therefore, I
recommend
checking your
cruise line's
guidelines
before
haphazardly
packing.

For some reason, there is a growing issue of people violating cruise line dress codes, especially the more formal ones, and it leaves the dining room personnel in a sticky situation. They don't want to upset guests by turning them away, but they also hesitate to anger those who have loyally adhered to the evening's guidelines. It's a conundrum.

The reason for having formal nights is to revisit the elegant ocean voyages of the past. Think of how everyone was dressed for dinner in the movie *Titanic* and what a big deal it was. That means people who don tuxedos and evening gowns are doing so with passion, and they frown upon those who don't respect the tradition.

Granted, a guy wearing shorts and a T-shirt on formal night will be asked to politely return to his cabin and reconsider his wardrobe choice. But, what happens if he shows up in a pair of Gucci dress jeans, an Ermenegildo Zegna button-down shirt, and woven Ferragamo loafers, sans the socks? That's a rather expensive outfit despite its dress code violation, and I feel for the maître d' who struggles with what to do. Fortunately, that very outfit is on the approved list for dress-up evenings on many lines these days. It just won't pass muster for formal or black-tie optional dress codes.

Again, check your cruise line's dress code before you pack. But, to get you started, here are some general guidelines for the various terms they might use:

Formal: Tuxedos or dinner jackets for men. Evening gowns, cocktail dresses, or dressy evening separates for women.

Black Tie Optional: Dark suits & ties or tuxedos for men. Evening gowns, cocktail dresses, or dressy evening separates for women.

Semiformal: Suits or jackets for men. Dresses or pantsuits for women.

Informal: Collared or button-down shirts for men with dress pants or smart trousers. Sport coats are optional. Blouses, sweaters, skirts, dresses or dressy slacks for women.

Evening Chic: This code is rather open-ended with no strict requirements, but the idea is to encourage passengers to step up the evening's dress with a little pizzazz. Think of a girls' night out at the club.

Elegant Casual: Slacks and collared shirts for men with jackets advised, but still optional. Ties are not required. Skirts or slacks with blouses or sweaters, pantsuits, or dresses for women.

Country Club Casual: Similar to Elegant Casual, but one step dressier. For men, think dressier slacks and jackets as more of a rule than an option. For women, lean toward styles, fabrics, shoes, etc. that are more upscale.

Smart Casual: Like Elegant Casual, but one step *less* dressy. Slacks, khakis, and open-necked shirts for men. Skirts, slacks, sweaters, pantsuits, and dresses for women.

Resort Casual: Upscale sportswear, golf attire, shorts, pants, and optional jackets for men. Upscale sportswear, shorts, casual dresses, skirts and pants for women.

Cruise Casual: Sport slacks, khakis, nice jeans, long dress shorts and collared sport shirts for men. Casual dresses, casual skirts or pants, blouses, summer dresses, Capri pants, dressy shorts, and nice jeans for women.

Casual: Khakis, tasteful jeans, dress shorts and collared sport shirts for men. Casual dresses, casual skirts or pants, casual tops, Capri pants, and tasteful jeans for women. Higher-quality unprinted crewneck shirts may also be allowed, but discretion is advised.

Some lines, like Oceania, have no formal nights and maintain Country Club Casual for the duration of the cruise. Azamara Club Cruises has formal nights, but formal wear is neither expected nor required, thereby giving hardcore traditional cruisers the opportunity to dress up if they are so inclined, but not setting their expectations that others will join in.

Most luxury and premium cruise lines that observe a permanent Country Club or Resort Casual dress code do not allow jeans, shorts, T-shirts, tank tops, halter tops, athletic footwear, or beach-type sandals in any public area after 6:00pm. On others, tasteful jeans may be allowed on casual nights and dress jeans on dressier nights.

Casual jeans with holes and frayed cuffs are generally discouraged on all lines for dinner or in the evening hours in public spaces.

Swimsuits, short shorts, cover-ups, exercise attire and beach-type sandals should only be worn poolside, on open upper decks, in the fitness center, and in the spa, though most non-luxury lines will allow these clothing items in the buffet restaurant during the day.

Enjoying All the Free Stuff

Cruise lines vary as to what's included in your cruise fare, and each ship has its own offerings, but you can bet that there will be plenty to do on board that won't cost you extra. We've already covered some of this in other sections, but let's do a recap of all the free stuff, add a few more items, and put it all together in one section for easy reference.

When it comes to **food**, you can count on eating for free in the main dining room and buffet restaurant, but you'll usually find other free venues like a pizza counter, a grill for burgers and dogs, the specialty coffee bar (pastries in the morning and small sandwiches later in the day), a soft-serve ice cream bar, and maybe even a specialty restaurant or two. For example, Guy's Burger Joint (a la Guy Fieri) serves scrumptious free burgers on Carnival ships, and Red Ginger on Oceania Cruises offers outstanding Asian fusion cuisine conceived by world-renowned chef Jacques Pépin. You can check out all the dining venues on your cruise, including which ones are free, by looking up your ship on the cruise line's website.

Live performances across the ship are almost always included in your cruise fare, from Broadway-style shows in the Main Theater to a jazz trio in an intimate lounge. Marquee performances in the larger entertainment venues may require reservations, so be sure to make yours online in advance of the cruise, but they usually don't require any sort of payment. Performances that aren't free usually include a meal, such as a dinner theater show like *Cirque Dreams* on Norwegian Cruise Lines.

Almost every Large Ship or Megaship offers an **outdoor movie venue**, such as Movies Under the Stars on Princess Cruises, where you can snuggle up in a blanket on a lounge chair with a bag of free popcorn to watch a recently released major motion picture.

When it comes to **activities**, especially on newer Megaships, it's surprising how many terrific facilities are free to use. The only hitch is having to wait in line to use them. Each ship has different offerings, but these may include ziplines, surf simulators, indoor skydiving, water slides, rock-climbing walls, miniature golf, bumper cars, go-carts, laser tag, a ropes course, a boardwalk carousel, and of course the selection of pools and hot tubs on board.

Speaking of pools and hot tubs, **adult-only retreats** are almost always free to use, thereby providing adult passengers with a quiet, kid-free environment to relax, swim, soak, read or enjoy a refreshing cocktail.

The onboard **fitness center**, with its array of machines and weights, are also free to use, although fitness classes may come with a small charge. There should also be a **sport court** for basketball or tennis as well as a **jogging track** on an upper deck or the Promenade deck.

Some cruise lines like Carnival, Celebrity and Princess (on some ships) allow free access to **saunas and steam rooms** in the spa facility without having to buy a treatment.

Art auctions can be a lot of fun to watch, even if you don't bid on anything, and it's enriching to browse all the beautiful paintings beforehand. Besides, the auctioneers usually pour **free Champagne** without pressuring anyone to bid or buy.

Of course, just being on a ship in the middle of the ocean is a treat of its own, and it's hard to beat the relaxation of sitting on a **deck chair or lounge** with a cup of coffee or glass of wine and watch the sea streaming by, the wake of the ship off the stern, or the sun setting over the water.

Planning Your Sea Days

No one wants to be overly structured while they're on vacation, but without a little strategic planning, it's easy for the days to get away from you on a cruise ship, and that leads to missing out on some of the fun. I have heard many people say their cruise was over before they knew it, and they never got around to enjoying some of the things they had intended to do on board.

It's also a little more complicated than just making a list of what you're going to do on Sea Day One and Sea Day Two. All live performances have feature times, and some recreational venues have operating hours, so you'll need to plan around those. And, if you don't want to wait in a long line for the super cool stuff like indoor skydiving and surf simulators, you should get there right when they open. Another option is to enjoy them on port days when most other passengers are on shore.

In addition, some venues transform into different uses at various times of day. For example, the SeaPlex on Royal Caribbean's *Quantum of the Seas* is set up for basketball or circus school (including a trapeze) during the day, but transforms into roller-skating, bumper cars or dancing in the evening and late-night hours. It's important to check your daily cruise program for the applicable hours for each.

If you're signed up for flexible dining or plan to visit the specialty restaurants, I recommend making your entertainment reservations first, then plan your dinner reservations around them

If you have teenagers who plan to use the more involved recreational facilities such as ziplining or rock climbing, you'll need to make time to accompany them at check-in and sign the release forms as their parent or legal guardian. If you have younger children who will be using day care or kid zones, you'll need to work around their operating hours and possibly make reservations for various services, such as having them picked up early at dinner to leave you and your spouse with a romantic evening on your own.

The pools are most crowded on sea days, so plan to get there early to snag a choice lounge chair for the day. Just don't leave it unattended for more than thirty minutes because cruise lines have started monitoring lounge chairs and will remove your belongings after half an hour of no activity, under the assumption you're "saving" it for later in the day, which isn't allowed. They'd rather make it available for someone who's ready to bask in the sun right away.

> **TIP:** If you're planning to spend time at the pool or on a deck lounge somewhere other than your balcony, pack a tote bag or backpack similar to the one you take on shore, thereby ensuring you have everything you need without having to constantly run back and forth to your stateroom.

CHAPTER 13: PORT DAYS

KEVIN STREUFERT

Sailing into Port and Docking

On most port days, your ship's scheduled arrival time will be relatively early, such as 6:00am to 8:00am, unless it takes longer to traverse the distance from the vessel's previous stop.

At larger ports, multiple ships may be coming in for the day, and the scheduled arrival times will be staggered to avoid congestion in the harbor as well as to allow dockworkers to move from one ship to the next as they assist them in tying up to the pier.

If you're up early enough to watch the whole procedure, you'll notice your ship sailing into the port 30 minutes or so prior to the scheduled arrival time, and it will slow to a crawl as it negotiates to the assigned pier. Your captain will use the azimuth thrusters to navigate sideways and square up to the dock, sometimes rotating 180 degrees before doing so. This latter procedure is the equivalent of backing a car into a parking space, thereby facilitating an easy exit when it's time to leave.

Once the ship is within 20 feet or so of the pier, the crew will "toss out" mooring lines, usually via automatic reels built into the bow and stern of the ship. Some of these ropes are so large that dockworkers use fork lifts to grab hold of the looped ends and lift them onto the massive horn cleats or bollards on the pier. Once secured, the crew slowly reels in the mooring lines, gradually tugging the ship the remaining few feet and firmly securing it against the dock bumpers.

Passenger and crew gangways are attached to (or extended from) the ship shortly thereafter, and passengers are allowed to disembark as soon as the local port authority has granted clearance. Once this occurs, an announcement will be made throughout the common areas that the ship is ready for debarkation. The broadcast will also identify the location of the passenger gangway and confirm when guests must be back on board.

If you wake up extra early, and your stateroom is on the correct side of the ship, you may see a pilot boat or tugboat when your ship is still some distance from land, and it will pull up to a small access door to offload a person. This is a licensed maritime pilot for that port of call, who joins the captain on the bridge and helps navigate the ship through the deep-water channels leading into the harbor itself. These pilots also typically help navigate the ship back out to open seas when the ship departs.

Getting Off and Back On the Ship

Every time you leave the ship, you will present your cruise card to a member of the security team, who will scan it and check your appearance against the photo that appears on his or her computer screen. This logs you off the ship, and the same process happens upon your return to log you back ON the ship. This way, the crew can keep track of any passengers who might not have made it back on board by the prescribed deadline.

The reverse is true on Debarkation Day, where the system is used to confirm when every passenger has finally left the ship (or at least every passenger who is *supposed* to leave the ship), thereby allowing the crew to work with immigration and the port authority to clear the vessel for boarding by the next set of passengers.

Why wouldn't all passengers leave the ship, you may ask? Because some people take back-to-back cruises or book long itineraries that may be a combination of several smaller ones. Consequently, not every passenger will be scheduled to leave at the end of your particular cruise. There's also a growing number of retirees living permanently on cruise ships in lieu of a less-expensive assisted living facility, and they may remain on board any given vessel for months at a time.

When you return to the ship from your shore excursion, you will be required to run any bags through an X-Ray machine and walk through a metal detector, just like on Embarkation Day. As noted earlier, any alcohol you purchased on shore and attempt to bring back on board will be taken from you, but it will be logged and stored so you can retrieve it at the end of the cruise.

> **TIP:** If you are re-boarding the ship at a foreign port of call, be prepared for an immigration and/or security checkpoint before you proceed to the ship. This may even duplicate the security screening you'll endure after stepping on board, including X-Ray and metal scans. At least you'll have peace of mind that your security and safety are a top priority.

What You Should Take with You

No matter what anyone else may tell you, always take your passport with you whenever you go on shore in a foreign country. Even if the ship's crew announces that "a driver's license is sufficient for this port", take your passport anyway. In the unlikely event an incident prevents you from rejoining your ship before its departure, you need that passport to travel to the ship's next port of call and get back on board. You also never know when you'll need the services of a US Embassy or Consulate, which may not admit you under heightened conditions if you aren't in possession of your passport. Essentially, any interaction you have with an authority in a foreign country will be far more easily facilitated with your passport in-hand.

Your cruise card (or token) is also essential, but you won't be able get off the cruise ship without one, so it's just a matter of keeping track of it while you're on shore. The foreign country's immigration checkpoint will usually inspect it along with your passport when you arrive back at the pier.

Bring your cell phone in case of an emergency, even if you didn't buy an international calling package. If you like, leave your phone off unless you need it. You might also find a spot with free Wi-Fi, like one of the ever-growing number of Starbucks locations around the world, and you can use your phone to catch up on emails for free instead of using the ship's not-so-free Internet.

Other items are a matter of common sense or personal preference, and I recommend bringing a tote bag or small backpack to carry them with you throughout the day. These may include maps of the area, sunscreen, hand sanitizer, face moisturizer, lip moisturizer, moisturizing eye drops, any important medications, pain relievers, a travel umbrella, camera or GoPro, binoculars, towels (if you're heading to the beach), and anything else that fits your lifestyle like ear buds, headphones, portable game systems, etc.

If you're prone to allergies, bring your favorite treatment(s) in case you unexpectedly react to something in the air, food or elsewhere. If you occasionally suffer from indigestion, bring antacids.

Finally, consult the weather forecast in your daily cruise program for the port of call and bring appropriate attire in case it gets too hot, too cold, rainy or snowy. In any location with potentially wide swings in temperatures, such as Alaska, make sure you can layer with lighter-weight garments. Wearing a T-shirt under a heavy coat won't do the trick.

TIP: You may have difficulties obtaining an important item while on shore, especially medications. The challenge will be further compounded if you don't speak the language. It doesn't hurt to bring them along, just in case.

Meeting Your Shore Excursion

If you're heading out on a cruise line shore excursion, tickets will be delivered to your stateroom, usually on Embarkation Day, with instructions to meet at a designated venue on the ship at a specific time. When you arrive, a crewmember will give you a color-coded sticker for your tour, to be placed on the outside of your clothing, and you will proceed inside the venue to wait for your tour group to be called.

People will probably be waiting for numerous shore excursions, and you will be instructed to sit with everyone for your tour. Once the operator is ready, your group will be released to depart the ship, and someone will direct you to the meeting place for your bus, boat, or walking tour guide.

If you're taking a third-party tour, you should have received a voucher via email with instructions regarding where and when to meet the tour operator. Head down to the gangway about 20 to 30 minutes in advance of the meeting time since lines to disembark are occasionally long. If your ship is anchored in the water, and you'll be taking a tender to shore, leave 45 minutes to an hour before your meeting time. Once off the ship (or tender), just head to the meeting point.

> **TIP:** If you are planning to roll the dice with a random tour operator or driver at the pier, I suggest heading out as early as possible. The most reputable-looking gents are scooped up first. Also, arrange with them to get back well in advance of the ship's departure time to ensure you don't miss it.

Free Things to Do in Port

Not every port warrants an organized shore excursion. Perhaps the local area isn't as exciting as the other ports of call on the cruise itinerary, thereby making it a good day to hang back on the ship for a spa treatment or to enjoy onboard recreational facilities  when they aren't crowded. But it's more often because of the walkability of interesting sights right from the pier, usually when the port facility is situated in the heart of town. In that case, you can just walk off the ship and **tour the area on your own** for free.

Sure, you can pay for someone to walk you around, and that may be appropriate in some cases. But there are plenty of instances where it makes sense to do your own research in advance, print off a walking map from the Internet (check the local tourism board's website), plan a tour route with the sights you'd like to see along the way, and enjoy the town at your own pace. You can even stop at a sidewalk café for a cappuccino, glass of wine, or a beer and continue the tour whenever you feel like it. The best part is that it didn't cost you anything except a little time on the Internet at home. Well, and that glass of Bordeaux.

If you'd like to make your self-guided tour a little more interesting, consider **Geocaching** – a GPS-driven treasure-hunting challenge you play with a free geocaching app on your phone. The idea is to find hidden containers (geocaches) all over the world filled with trinkets. Take one for yourself, leave one behind, and sign the box's log book before you head off to find the next one.

Another option, although not exactly free, is to use a **walking tour app** like Field Trip, Historypin, Stray Boots, or Cities Talking. In this case, you have the benefit of a tour guide who tells you all about the sights you're seeing, but you can still take things at your own pace. If you're traveling as a couple and using wired earbuds or headphones, consider adding a Y-adapter so both of you can listen to the narration together on the same phone.

In addition to seeing the landmarks and other sights of a port city during your visit, you can **window shop** to your heart's content at the boutiques and markets, usually located nearby.

Cruise ports and the tourist areas surrounding them are also a magnet for **live street entertainment**, offering everything from music and magic to acrobatics and animated statues. While it may not be free to toss a contribution into a musician's open guitar case, it's a nice thing to do if you enjoy their performance.

If you're in a tropical location, you may be able to walk or take a free shuttle to the **beach** and enjoy a free day frolicking in the sun, sand and surf, usually with beachside restaurants and bars at the ready. Worst case scenario is that you pay a modest fare for a taxi driver to take you there, but be sure to ask him or her to return for you a couple of hours before your ship leaves port. If the driver doesn't show, that leaves you with plenty of time to find another option.

At some destinations in Alaska, Hawaii, Australia, New Zealand, South America and Southeast Asia, your port may be within walking distance of **hiking trails**. You can use an app like AllTrails to check what may be available near your port of call.

If you're a runner or jogger, consider skipping the onboard jogging track and **go for a run** on shore. There are plenty of online resources and apps to find safe, established routes in just about every port.

> **TIP:** GPS-based phone apps will use location services to navigate, which usually don't cost anything, but it's important to ensure these apps don't secretly use expensive roaming cellular data while you're touring around in a foreign country. Turn OFF Data Roaming on your phone to ensure that won't happen. Note that GPS will not work in Airplane Mode.

CHAPTER 14: DEBARKATION AND THE NIGHT BEFORE

Luggage Procedures

Trust me when I say you'll want the ship's porters to take any large suitcases off the ship for you, as it may be burdensome to carry them yourself. For example, my family and I experienced an issue upon disembarking a ship where the elevators were blocked from accessing the gangway level, and even

the deck above that. So, it became necessary to lug our carry-on bags down multiple flights of stairs.

You will be required to place your checked suitcases in the hallway outside your stateroom door the last night of the cruise, so hold back a carry-on or medium-sized roller bag to pack up anything you need until the following morning, including the outfit you're wearing that evening as you dance the night away.

Early on the last full day of the cruise, color-coded luggage tags designating your assigned departure group will be delivered to your stateroom. These should be attached to your suitcases before you place them out in the hallway. You will receive instructions regarding the deadline for doing this, which could be as early as 10:00pm or as late as 2:00am on Debarkation Morning.

If you haven't been provided with enough baggage tags, you can ask your cabin steward or the Passenger Services Desk for more. For information about changing your departure group, see **Getting Off the Ship** later in this chapter.

Once you arrive in the port building, your suitcases will be waiting for you in an area marked with your departure group number, and you can grab them before proceeding through immigration and customs. If you have too many bags to manage on your own, porters and/or luggage carts should be there to help you transport everything all the way to your mode of transportation.

Settling Your Onboard Account

During the final evening of the cruise, a detailed record of your shipboard account including every single charge or credit during the sailing will be delivered to your stateroom. This is your opportunity to review the account to see if any credits are missing or if you don't recognize some of the charges. You may also be able to review the account on your stateroom TV, and you can always go through it with the desk clerks at the Passenger Services Desk or your Suite concierge (if applicable).

Shipboard account errors are uncommon these days given the level of technology and controls in place, but it doesn't hurt to review everything just in case, especially if the total looks out of whack. Just remember that we all tend to make charges late at night that might not immediately come to mind. A review of the account may come with the words "oh, that's right" muttered over and over.

If you've provided a credit card to automatically settle your account, there's nothing else to do. After you've logged off the ship with your cruise card on Debarkation Day, confirming that you're done making last minute purchases like specialty coffees and Bloody Marys, your credit card will be charged the final balance.

If you're paying cash, you'll need to settle up with the Passenger Services Desk early on Debarkation Day or the night before. Once your shipboard account is closed out, you won't be able to make any further purchases.

Disembarking the Ship

Coordinating the departure of hundreds, if not thousands, of passengers in a relatively short amount of time is a daunting task. Inevitable bottlenecks occur, especially at the gangway where security personnel are scanning cruise cards and checking photos as fast as they can. Some cruise lines (and individual ships) do a better job than others at managing the chaos, but be prepared to spend some time in line, especially during the earlier hours of the morning as passengers rush to leave, sometimes before their designated departure time.

For this reason, I suggest arranging a late departure on Debarkation Day. You may have a deadline for vacating your stateroom to allow the steward time to service it for the next guest, but you can still find a place to relax, have a leisurely breakfast, enjoy an extra cup of coffee or tea, and have a nice chat while everyone else scrambles to leave. Cruise lines like Celebrity have even started offering late, VIP debarkation privileges (for a charge), which allow you to stay on board, have lunch, and wait until 90 minutes or so before the ship sets sail again to finally disembark.

As mentioned in the last section, your cabin steward will deliver color-coded luggage tags marked with your assigned departure group and an estimated timetable for each group's departure. This assignment is based upon information you provided to the cruise line during your online check-in, most specifically your return flight itinerary. If your flight is late in the day or on a following day, you will be assigned to a later departure group. If your flight is before Noon, your group will be one of the first to leave. The crew also considers the departure time of any post-cruise tours and prioritize those passengers to ensure they reach the tour vehicle on time.

If you leave before your group is called, your checked luggage may not be available in the port building when you arrive there. Baggage deliveries are queued with each group's departure time, which incentivizes people to cooperate with the timetable and stage their departures to avoid a bottleneck. In reality, bags are delivered just before each corresponding group is officially called, meaning they will sit there while the group makes its way off the ship. That can take 30 minutes or longer, and experienced cruisers often leave half an hour early, thereby causing the very bottlenecks the crew is trying to avoid.

If you receive a group assignment that's too late to accommodate your plans, such as an early flight, the Passenger Services Desk (or your Concierge, if applicable) will be happy to provide you with baggage tags for an earlier group. Don't worry if you've been assigned to an *earlier* group than you need because no one is going to force you to get off the ship at the designated time. Your checked bags will still be waiting for you in the cruise terminal when you get there. You can feel free to disembark at your leisure, just as long as you've left your stateroom by the deadline and scampered off the ship no later than the final departure group.

If you would prefer to leave early and beat the crowds, try packing light and opting for the "Self-Assist" or "Walk-Off" option, whereby you agree to carry all your own bags, potentially down stairs and ramps. This group is usually the first to be called for departure, and you can beat the long lines. You will also have the option to depart at your leisure without worrying about unattended bags inside the cruise terminal.

CHAPTER 15: RIVER CRUISING

Introduction

As I mentioned at the beginning of this book, river cruises are less involved than ocean voyages, hence the single chapter on the subject. However, there are still a few choice things you should know before you book or embark on a river cruise vacation. Let's go over those now.

We'll use the same methodical process as we did with ocean cruises, but on a smaller scale. First, I'll help familiarize you with river cruises in general, including their unique ships, staterooms, procedures and characteristics.

Then, we'll move on to the most common itineraries river cruise lines offer, segregated by the waterways they navigate. This information should assist you in deciding whether a river cruise is right for you and help establish where you'd like to go.

That will leave the task of selecting a river cruise line, and I'll provide a one-page summary of each major player, just like I did with the ocean cruise lines, giving you a sense of which operators fit you the best.

We won't go over the selection process again because it's effectively the same as ocean cruises. You should be able to incorporate what you learn here into that methodology. Then, either call your travel agent or book your perfect river cruise online.

The River Cruise Difference

Without question, river cruises offer a few advantages over ocean cruises. The first is the ability to directly access towns and cities that ocean vessels can't get to. The only other feasible way to visit all these places would be to travel by bus or car, staying in multiple hotels, constantly packing and unpacking your belongings along the way. I don't know about you, but that doesn't sound very relaxing to me

River cruises tend to be more inclusive than ocean cruises, usually with things like alcohol (or at least beer & wine with dinner), most shore excursions, WiFi, and even the onshore use of bicycles being complimentary.

Another significant difference between river and ocean cruises is how they are structured. In fact, they are almost backwards from each other. Ocean cruise ships usually sail overnight, arrive at the next port in the morning, and stay until the evening. They'll also mix in a few days at sea. River cruises, on the other hand, almost always sail during some portion of the day or evening and stay in port overnight, thereby allowing passengers to see the beautiful scenery and riverside towns along the way. They also hit at least one port each day, with a selection of excursion options, meaning that you're always on the go. In other words, say goodbye to those relaxing sea days when you sleep late, have a spa treatment, relax by the pool, and drink wine on your balcony for hours while you watch the sea go by.

The length of an ocean cruise can be anywhere from 3 to 100 days or more, whereas river cruises typically last 7 days, although some lines, like Crystal, start at 10. Fortunately, the shorter cruise length allows for more time to be spent in the pre- and post-cruise cities, which are usually worth an entire vacation on their own.

River cruises face different challenges than ocean vessels, too. For example, itineraries can be canceled, interrupted or altered because of flooding, which causes the river to rise too high for the ship to fit under bridges. The same is true with drought conditions, when the water is too low to accommodate the vessel in the river at all. In either of these cases, it is not uncommon for the cruise line to send passengers to the ports of call by motorcoach and either put them up in hotels or transfer them to another ship to continue the voyage.

River cruise ships (discussed in the next section) are small and intimate, with fewer guests and highly personalized service. You also won't experience ocean-cruise crowds when getting on and off the vessel.

Most of the entertainment on river cruises consists of enrichment lectures, often focused on cultural immersion in the destination, and modest musical acts, which frequently come on board for the evening to perform while the ship is in port.

Gourmet cuisine is also a common element on river cruises, with some lines taking the concept to greater heights than others. Nevertheless, it's safe to say that any river cruise ship from the lines listed later in this chapter will have fantastic food. That's because the small number of guests eliminates the need for an institutional kitchen, allowing chefs to create handcrafted dishes with personal attention, just like a gourmet restaurant on land.

It is also *de rigueur* for the ship's executive chef to source local, fresh ingredients at the ports of call for onboard meals. You might even be able to join him or her in lieu of a shore excursion to shop at the local markets for produce, fish, meats and spices.

River Cruise Ships

River cruise ships are designed specifically for the waterways on which they sail, ensuring they fit into the applicable locks and underneath every bridge. Some vessels have top-deck features and  even full-fledged venues that disappear into the deck while traversing under bridges that are particularly low. Don't worry if you're sitting at a bar that's about to vanish because someone will make sure you move!

Due to the size limitations of a vessel that can legally and successfully traverse a river, even the largest of river cruise ships are small. That means a limited number of staterooms, fewer guests, and by default a more personalized cruise experience. Crewmembers get to know you by name in no time, and you can't help but become acquainted with your fellow guests, making new friends along the way.

The downside to the size restrictions is a limited number of onboard venues, from specialty restaurants and performance halls to bars and expansive pool decks. But that's not the point of a river cruise, and no one misses them. Most river cruise lines do a fine job with dining choices, a variety of lounges with intimate seating areas, entertainment options, and roomy sun decks with plenty of lounges and an enjoyable pool.

River cruise ships also rarely experience sea turbulence, for obvious reasons, so they are ideal vessels for people with motion-sickness concerns.

River Cruise Staterooms

It seems intuitive that a river cruise ship stateroom would be significantly smaller than an ocean cruise ship stateroom. However, when you compare apples to apples, such as one oceanview cabin to another, they're not all that different. Granted, you won't find as many huge suites on a river cruise vessel, but that's because there's already a limited amount of space to fit in the smaller staterooms most people want, much less adding a selection of space-hogging owner's suites. If a suite is your preference, they do exist on river ships and can be reasonably large, including a few with two bedrooms.

Balconies on river cruise ships are a different story. Because of the narrow width of the vessel, the best way to maximize the size of the stateroom is to incorporate a French balcony rather than the full walk-out balconies you find on oceangoing ships. In most cases, the French balcony is accessed by a large sliding-glass door or exceptionally large window that disappears into the wall, thereby opening the cabin to the outside air and creating the closest thing possible to a "real" balcony—handrail and all. Still, some cruise lines like AmaWaterways offer staterooms with real balconies, which eat into the interior space and necessitate taking up more of the deck's "footprint" to achieve the desired square footage of the cabin itself.

Otherwise, river cruise ship staterooms are similar to their ocean ship counterparts with the exception of the standard luxury factor. By and large, river cruises are more expensive than ocean cruises, so passengers expect their accommodations to reflect that increase in cost. This is also due to the high-quality benchmarks set by the cruise lines that pioneered the river cruise industry, and every competitor to this day must meet at least the minimum in luxury standards to compete.

You can expect the cabin's bathroom to be similar to an ocean version as well, with a small shower, a vacuum-operated toilet, and a modest countertop & sink. Still, it will be perfectly functional, and the décor will most likely fit with the high-end nature of the cabin itself. Super-luxury river cruise bathrooms are often decked in marble and feature all the amenities you would expect from a 5-star hotel.

River Cruise Regions

Here are the major river cruise regions, broken out by their cruise-worthy waterways. For each river, I have identified the cities and/or countries you may visit along the way, but each cruise line offers different itineraries, so you'll need to search for the one that appeals to you the most. As with ocean cruises, a particular itinerary may ultimately sway you toward one cruise line over another.

Europe

River cruises through Europe offer a feast for the eyes and the soul, with rich landscapes, charming villages, magnificent castles, and sprawling vineyards along the way. As the birthplace of Western Civilization, Europe offers a fascinating look into our own history, with culturally significant sites at every turn. When it comes to art, food and wine, there isn't another destination in the world that can possibly compare.

Rhine

The Rhine begins in the Swiss town of Graubünden, flows through Western Germany, and ultimately empties into the North Sea in the Netherlands. It touches Austria, France and Liechtenstein along the way.

Most Rhine river cruises span between Basel at the south end and Amsterdam to the north. Typical stops include Strasbourg in France, Kinderdijk in the Netherlands, and the German towns of Cologne (Köln), Heidelberg, Mannheim, Koblenz, Breisach, Speyer and Rüdesheim. The collection of historical sites, churches, charming villages, and fascinating architecture is beyond compare.

The Rhine is mostly known for the vineyards and castles along its banks, offering cruise passengers a sumptuous visual experience and the opportunity to sample delicious wines every step along the way.

Danube

The romantic Danube flows through ten different countries. It originates in Germany's Black Forest before flowing southeast to pass through or touch Austria, Slovakia, Hungary,  Croatia, Serbia, Romania, Bulgaria, Moldova, and finally the Ukraine, where it terminates into the Black Sea.

Still, Danube river cruises usually don't travel farther south than Budapest, Hungary, either starting or ending there, with Vilshofen or Nuremburg (in Germany) representing the opposite end of a typical 7-day voyage. Longer itineraries merge with the Main and Rhine rivers to provide passage as far as Amsterdam.

In addition to the beginning and ending points mentioned above, stops along a Danube-only river cruise may include Vienna, Krems, Dürnstein, Linz and Melk in Austria, often with an optional side-trip to Salzburg. Bratislava (Slovakia) is another popular stop, as are the German towns of Passau and Regensburg, perhaps with a side trip to Munich. For oenophiles, visiting the Wachau Valley Wine Region is a highlight.

Elbe

Rising in the Krkonoše Mountains near Poland, the Elbe flows across the Czech Republic before traversing Germany on its way to the town of Cuxhaven, northwest of Hamburg, where it empties into the North Sea.

Most cruises on the Elbe only go as far as Wittenberg or Magdeburg to the northwest, with motorcoach service to and from Berlin and Potsdam. Toward the southeast, cruises stop at Melnik or Děčín, both of which offer an easy connection to Prague.

Stops in between include Dresden, Dessau, Meissen, Torgau, Bad Schandau and Litoměřice. An optional transfer to Warsaw, Poland may also be available, with tour stops in Kraków and Czestochowa along the way.

Cruises on the Elbe aren't as commonplace as those on the other major European rivers, but they provide a look into unique cultural, historical and architectural wonders that many people will never have an opportunity to see. They are a fine selection for well-traveled individuals looking for something new.

Seine

Many people think of Paris and all its romantic bridges when the Seine is mentioned, and that's where most river cruises on this waterway begin and end.

The Seine originates at Source-Seine, northwest of Dijon, before heading through Paris and ending in Le Havre at the English Channel.

Round-trip Paris cruises to Normandy are the most common, with potential stops in Rouen, Giverny (Monet's home), Vernon, Conflans, Les Andelys, and Mantes-la-Jolie along the way. Usually, a selection of shore excursions to the Normandy Beaches, monuments, cemeteries and other installations are included or otherwise available.

Rhône

The Rhône river rises from the Rhône Glacier in the Swiss Alps near Valais and runs through Lake Geneva before passing through southeastern France to the Mediterranean Sea. In Arles, shortly before the river reaches the Mediterranean, it splits into two branches known as Le Grand Rhône and Le Petit Rhône.

River cruises on the Rhône typically run between Lyon at the north end and Avignon (in Provence) at the south, where easy side trips to Arles and Les Baux are the norm. Stops in between may include Vienne, Tournon, Collonges, Viviers, and possibly a jaunt up to Mâcon via the Saône River.

These cruises are often wine-focused with the opportunity to experience selections from Beaujolais, Côtes du Rhône and the Rhône Valley.

Garonne, Dordogne & Gironde

The Garonne and its estuaries are ideal gateways to the Bordeaux region, with its exquisite wines and many beautiful chateaux.

Most ships sail round-trip from the city of Bordeaux and visit legendary port towns like Saint-Émilion, Cadillac, Pauillac, Bourg, Blaye, and Libourne. If you are so inclined, you may have the choice of taking a side trip to Bergerac or Cognac.

Clearly, these river cruises are more about the wines than the destinations, with tastings and winery visits at every turn. Still, don't miss the beautiful landscape, historical sites, superb architecture and charming towns along the way.

Douro

Without question, the Douro is a hidden treasure that hasn't popped up on most travelers' radar screens. Its source lies near the town of Duruelo de la Sierra, from which it sets out to traverse northern-central Spain and Portugal to its Atlantic Ocean outlet in Porto.

Here, one visits charming towns with unfamiliar names like Vega de Terrón, Pinhão, Lamego, Entre-os-Rios, Mateus, Barca d'Alva and Régua. The trip features a splendid collection of breathtaking gorges, romantic vineyards, and sleepy little fishing villages that unexpectedly satisfy the heart and soul.

Most cruises sail round-trip from Porto and offer an excursion to the fascinating town of Salamanca in Spain (a UNESCO World Heritage Site) at the turn.

Russia and the Ukraine

When it comes to choosing a river cruise, most people don't think about Russia or the Ukraine. But a further investigation into the region's passion and rich treasures might change their minds.

A cruise through these areas satisfies the quest for exploration and brings a sense of enlightenment and understanding that helps bridge the gap between our peoples and cultures.

Neva, Svir & Volga

The gold standard of river cruises in Russia sail from St. Petersburg to Moscow, with opportunities to experience both of these remarkable cities as well as the non-touristy local culture in between. These cruises not only traverse the Neva, Svir and Volga rivers, but travel across Lake Ladoga, Lake Onega and the Rybinsk Reservoir.

Stops along the way are towns we've never heard of like Mandrogi, Kizhi, Kuzino, Goritsi, Yaroslavl and Uglich. Here, one can immerse themselves in authentic Russian culture by sharing a meal with a local family, sampling Russian caviar, visiting a traditional steam bath (Banya), listening to folk music, or enjoying vodka like a native.

In St. Petersburg and Moscow, one can visit heralded sites like Catherine's Palace, the Hermitage, the Kremlin, Saint Basil's Cathedral, and the Church of the Savior on Spilled Blood.

Dnieper

In the Ukraine, cruises on the Dnieper River run between Kiev and Odessa, at which point it flows into the Black Sea. The river actually originates much farther north in Smolensk, Russia and crosses Belarus before transitioning into a major waterway in the Ukraine, where it has served as a trade route for centuries.

Ports of call on Dnieper river cruises usually include Kremenchug, Dnipro, Zaporozhye, and Kherson. There are numerous historic sites, onion-domed churches and cultural immersion opportunities along the way, with the highlights being Kiev's Cave Monasteries, Odessa's Potemkin Steps, and demonstrations by skilled Cossack horsemen.

Asia

Ocean cruises around Southeast Asia open up a world of fascinating destinations, historical sites and artifacts. Here's your chance to explore some of the interior along the waterways of China, Vietnam and Cambodia.

Yangtze

The historically significant Yangtze River in China is the longest in Asia. It provides drainage for one-fifth of the land area of the People's Republic of China, and its river basin serves as home to one-third of the country's population. It is the largest river in the

world to flow entirely within a single country. There's a lot to see along this waterway, with plenty of dramatic natural scenery to add to the fascinating cultural immersion opportunities.

Cruises along the Yangtze typically run between Chongqing on the west end and Yichang or Wuhan to the east. They usually serve as one component of a larger cruisetour package with flights to Shanghai and Beijing on either end, allowing travelers to experience many of the gems of China including the Great Wall, Forbidden City, Temple of Heaven, and Xian's Terra Cotta Army. Longer itineraries may include a jaunt over to Tibet for a taste of its sacred treasures like Jokhang Temple, Potala Palace and Sera Monastery.

These short cruises pass through the Yangtze's spectacular Three Gorges, which garnered worldwide attention after construction of the Three Gorges Dam, completed in 2006. The dam has dramatically changed the river and continues to have a significant effect on the region's people and ecology, including numerous villages and archeological sites that are now located under water.

Mekong

Beginning at the Tibetan Plateau, the Mekong is a trans-boundary river that runs through or borders China's Yunnan Province, Myanmar (Burma), Laos and Thailand before reaching Cambodia and Vietnam, where it empties into the South China Sea.

River itineraries go as far as Kampon Cham in Cambodia to the north and Ho Chi Minh City in Vietnam to the south. Stops along the way often include Kampong Cham, Ankor Ban and Phnom Penh in Cambodia as well as Tân Châu, Sa Đéc, Cai Be, Vinh Long, Gieng Island and Evergreen Island in Vietnam. Cruisetour destinations or side trips are usually available to Angkor Wat and Siem Reapp, where flight transfers to and from Hanoi are also available.

The highlights of a Mekong cruise include small, unspoiled river towns, lush scenery, fascinating religious sites, truly unique architecture, and the opportunity to experience an entirely unfamiliar culture by interacting with the people, shopping in waterfront markets, taking a rickshaw ride through town, and listening to stories told by the locals.

Irrawaddy

The Irrawaddy River is the largest and most important commercial waterway in the country of Myanmar (Burma). It rises from the confluence of the N'mai and Mali Rivers before flowing southward through Myanmar until emptying into the Andaman Sea. It is sometimes referred to as "The Road to Mandalay", in reference to the chorus of Rudyard Kipling's famous poem.

Cruises on the Irrawaddy can last 3 to 14 days, depending on the distance traveled. Most sail between Mandalay and Bagan (the country's capital), but others may travel through the upper

Irrawaddy as far north as Bhamo. Additional ports of call may include Shwe Pyi Thar, Amarapura, Sagaing, Kyauk Myaung, Kya Hnyat, Tigyang, Katha, and Kyn Daw. Most cruisetours begin in Yangon (formerly Rangoon) with a compulsory visit to the gilded Shwedagon Pagoda (pictured), followed by a flight to reach the embarkation point for the cruise.

Clearly one of the most fascinating locales in the world, Myanmar offers mesmerizing energy and opulent, otherworldly treasures that sometimes defy belief. A cruise on the Irrawaddy offers an ideal way to immerse oneself into the culture, including the fascinating Burmese people, and provide splendid views of the beautiful natural wonders along the way.

Africa

A river/land cruisetour is an ideal choice for visiting the interior of Africa and experiencing its countless historical treasures, not to mention its fierce and graceful wildlife.

Nile

Generally considered to be the longest river in the world (though recent evidence proves the Amazon to be longer), the north-flowing Nile runs through eleven African countries including Egypt, Ethiopia, Sudan, Uganda, Congo-Kinshasa, Kenya, Tanzania, Rwanda, Burundi, South Sudan and Eritrea. The northern section of the river flows almost entirely through Egypt before terminating into the Mediterranean Sea.

Most river cruises on the Nile are round-trip sailings out of Luxor, but they are usually part of a cruisetour with transfers to and from Cairo, a city worthy of multiple days of exploration on its own. Cairo is also the gateway to the Pyramids of Giza, Great Sphinx, and countless other treasures in or around the ancient capital of Memphis.

Ports of call during the river cruise often include Dendera, Kom Ombo, Abu Simbel, Aswan, Wadi el Seboua, and Edfu. Massive statuary, stunning temples, important archeological sites and bustling markets abound on this journey, and you can count on plenty of local music, delicacies, lectures and interactions with the locals to provide a thorough cultural immersion.

Chobe

Depending on where you come across it in south-central Africa, the Chobe River may be known by one of four different names, with others being the Cuando, the Linyanti, and the Zambesi. In its entirety, the river rises at the plateau of Angola on the  slopes of Mount Tembo and flows mostly as swamps and marshes through or along the countries of Zambia, Angola, Namibia, Botswana, Zimbabwe and Mozambique. It becomes the Chobe River after passing through the seasonal lake of Liambesi, where it is suitable for cruising. The river ultimately empties into the Indian Ocean after crossing Mozambique as the Zambezi.

The primary goal of a cruise on the Chobe is to view Africa's sensational wildlife, and many safari-type opportunities are offered via boat, barge, and open-topped 4x4. Visiting a typical African village is another common excursion, giving passengers the opportunity to interact with the local children and elders. After the cruise, it's an easy visit to stunning Victoria Falls and the natural beauty surrounding it.

Most Chobe river cruises serve as part of an overall cruisetour that includes time in Cape Town and Johannesburg as well as Victoria Falls.

India

River cruises in India offer a unique way to explore the country's exotic treasures, and they integrate well with cruisetours that add other must-see locales such as the Golden Triangle of New Delhi, Jaipur and Agra (home of the Taj Mahal).

Ganges

The Ganges is a trans-boundary river that rises from the Himalayas before traversing India and Bangladesh, where it ultimately flows into the Bay of Bengal. The river is sacred to Hindus, and it serves as a lifeline to millions of people in India.

In actuality, Ganges river cruises operated by Western companies run on its southern distributaries—the Hooghly, Jalangi and Bhagirathi Rivers—in West Bengal, India. But, they are all part of the Ganges Delta and considered by locals to be one and the same. These are referred to as "Lower Ganges Cruises", and they usually sail round trip from Kolkata with stops in small towns and villages with names like Kalna, Matiari, Murshidabad, Baranagar, Mayapur, Bandel and Chandannagar.

A river cruise on the Ganges is not for everyone. Yes, there will be numerous excursions to visit temples and other interesting cultural sites, with friendly and engaging people wherever you go. But, the people and settlements along the river reveal extreme poverty and a shocking lack of hygiene, with copious amounts of trash as well as human and animal waste. Western cruise lines do a fine job of managing the situation, steering passengers away from certain areas and taking measures to clean and disinfect as frequently as possible. Still, there's only so much they can do. Travelers should prepare themselves and do their best to overlook the conditions in order to fully experience this mysterious and fascinating part of the world.

North America

For most people reading this book, a river cruise in North America is just a hop, skip and jump away. It not only saves on travel costs, but offers the opportunity for deeper exposure to one's own land, especially since shore excursions and onboard lectures tend to focus on cultural immersion and education.

Mississippi

The great Mississippi flows entirely in the United States, originating in Minnesota before meandering through or along ten states until finally emptying into the Gulf of Mexico, just south of New Orleans. It's literary and historical significance to the very fabric of the United

States is of legendary proportions.

Of course, a quintessential Mississippi river cruise happens on a paddlewheel riverboat, and there are plenty in operation to this day. Newer vessels may look the same, but they are fancier and full of creature comforts, bringing them in line with modern cruising in general. Itineraries may consist of a round-trip cruise out of New Orleans, the Lower Mississippi route from New Orleans to Memphis, the Middle Mississippi route between Memphis and St. Louis, and the Upper Mississippi route from St. Louis to St. Paul. Each segment usually takes 7 days, but you can take anywhere from 15 to 21 days to sail the full river from New Orleans to St. Paul (or in reverse). A few other itineraries venture onto the Ohio or Cumberland Rivers to reach Pittsburg or Nashville.

Other than the cities mentioned above, typical ports of call include Baton Rouge, Natchez, Vicksburg, Hannibal, Davenport, Dubuque, La Crosse, and Red Wing. Longer itineraries will add a number of smaller riverfront towns as well.

These cruises are port intensive with limited downtime, yet are still relaxing and casual. Entertainment usually consists of enrichment lectures and informal local entertainers.

Columbia & Snake

The Columbia River is the largest river in the Pacific Northwest. It originates in the Rocky Mountains of British Columbia, then flows through the state of Washington until reaching Oregon. There, it turns westward and forms most of the border between the two states before emptying into the Pacific Ocean. The Columbia's largest tributary is the Snake River, which continues eastward at Kennewick, Washington when the Columbia turns north, hence why most cruise itineraries include both waterways.

Most lines here offer river sailings between Astoria, Oregon and Clarkston, Washington. Eastbound itineraries typically embark in Portland, head west to Astoria, then backtrack to the east before traversing the greater part of a 500-mile route that passes through eight different locks.

Cruises on the Columbia and Snake Rivers focus on three primary draws. The first, of course, is the area's breathtaking beauty from Mount St. Helens and Multnomah Falls to the Columbia River Gorge and the lush vineyards of the Willamette Valley. The second is wine, for which the Pacific Northwest has become world-renowned, with Oregon Pinot Noir getting things off to a great start. Concentrated, wine-themed cruises are becoming ever-more popular here. Third is the fascinating historical significance of the Lewis and Clark expedition in the early 1800s, which followed the same route along these two rivers and fuels many of the onboard enrichment lectures.

St. Lawrence

At its origin, the St. Lawrence River is fueled by Lake Ontario. From there, it begins a northeast journey through the Canadian provinces of Quebec and Ontario until mingling with the Gulf of St. Lawrence and the Atlantic Ocean. The

river also forms part of the international boundary between Ontario, Canada and the US state of New York.

Because of its size, depth and accessibility from the Atlantic, sailings on the St. Lawrence consist of both river and ocean cruises. Small to Midsized cruise ships can sail all the way down the St. Lawrence from the Atlantic as part of a one-way Canada & New England cruise out of Boston, New York or Portland. The river isn't deep enough to accommodate Large ships and Megaships.

Given the various types of cruises and the assortment of vessels that sail them, this is one river without a "typical" itinerary. Still, there are common ports of call along the actual river and gulf that many ships will visit. Cruises typically start (or end) in either Montreal or Quebec City, with the other city often becoming a stop during the cruise.

Depending on the length of the itinerary, other ports of call may include Trois-Rivières, Prince Edward Island, Newfoundland, Nova Scotia, the Magdalen Islands, and possibly even some of the little riverside towns like Baie-Comeau, Sept-Iles, Gaspe, Havre-Saint-Pierre, and Saguenay (on the Saguenay River, which merges into the St. Lawrence).

Whether confined to the river itself or part of an ocean voyage, St. Lawrence cruises are appealing for so many reasons. The decidedly French culture with British influences gives one the feel of being in Europe, which is particularly evident in the architecture and lifestyles in Montreal and Quebec City. These cosmopolitan cities are full of fascinating people, rich histories, notable museums, beautiful churches, excellent restaurants, and many other sites of interest to tourists.

The river offers abundant natural beauty, from lush landscapes to dramatic cliffs, and its collection of marine life is fun to watch, particularly the many species of resident whales. But, the *pièce de résistance* is the breathtaking foliage in the fall.

South America

River cruises in South America are focused on the Amazon, and they are quite different from itineraries in Europe or the United States. This is jungle territory, with remarkable land, airborne and marine life at almost every turn.

Amazon

In 2014, a pair of American scientists performed a study that corrected the origin of the mighty Amazon River, changing what had been widely believed for almost a century. The most distant source is now known to be drainage from the Mantaro River in Peru, which adds almost 50 miles to the Amazon's length and makes it the longest river in the world, not to mention the largest by discharge rate. From Peru, the Amazon flows eastward, clipping the southeast corner of Colombia before traversing Brazil, where it empties into the Atlantic Ocean at a mind-boggling rate of 7.4 million cubic feet per second.

Amazon cruises take place on river sections either in Peru or Brazil. Naturally, with ocean access only on the Brazil side, that's where ocean cruise ships will take you, and the river's depth will accommodate some substantial vessels. The Amazon river cruise segment is usually part of a more extensive itinerary, such as a Caribbean and/or South American sailing out of Ft. Lauderdale, Miami or Rio de Janeiro. Ocean cruise ships go as far inland on

the river as Manaus, a whopping 1,000 miles away from the Atlantic, with stops at interesting riverside towns in both directions.

Cruises on the Peruvian side of the Amazon are offered on much smaller river ships maxing out at roughly 50 guests. These 3 to 7-day voyages sail round-trip out of Iquitos after a flight from Lima (or Nauta after an added drive from Iquitos) and are often part of a cruisetour package that includes Lima, Machu Picchu, Cusco, and the Sacred Valley. The river cruise portion focuses heavily on wildlife-viewing excursions, and there's plenty of local food, wine and cocktails on board.

RIVER CRUISE LINES

AmaWaterways

Founded	2002
Headquarters	Calabasas, CA
Ownership	Private
Destinations	Europe, Africa, Vietnam, Cambodia, Myanmar (Burma)
Languages	English, German
Caters to	North America, UK and Australia
Known for	Dual-balcony staterooms, gourmet regional cuisine, local wine & beer with meals, exceptional service, free tours
Dining	Main dining room with open seating and a complimentary specialty restaurant
Evening Attire	Smart Casual
Formal Nights	Captain's Dinner - Dressy
Slogan	*"Leading the Way in River Cruising"*

Summary

AmaWaterways' custom-designed ships carry an average of 150 passengers and feature larger-than-average, luxurious staterooms. In Europe, they cruise the Danube, Rhine, Main, Rhone, Seine, Douro and Mosel rivers, including wine-themed cruises focusing on local selections. AmaWaterways also cruises rivers in Africa, Vietnam, Cambodia and Myanmar (Burma). Fares include cuisine, wine & beer with meals, specialty coffees, bottled water, WiFi, in-room movies/entertainment, bicycles, and tours at every stop. Newer ships feature a unique dual-balcony design, with higher-end staterooms offering a French balcony as well as an outside veranda with two chairs. Each ship offers an expansive sundeck up top with intimate seating areas to gather and socialize.

Why Choose AmaWaterways?

AmaWaterways is known for its exceptionally high rate of customer satisfaction and attention to every detail. Considering the quality of their ships, superior service and fine cuisine, their cruise fares are a particularly good value for the discerning traveler.

American Cruise Lines

Founded	1991
Headquarters	Guilford, CT
Ownership	Private
Destinations	United States
Languages	English
Caters to	Older, North American citizens
Known for	Low-key atmosphere, evening lectures, regionally sourced and themed cuisine, large staterooms
Dining	Main dining room with open seating
Evening Attire	Casual Resort Attire
Formal Nights	None
Slogan	*"Small Ship Cruising Done Perfectly"*

Summary

With its small fleet of standard and paddle-wheeler riverboats, American Cruise Lines offers river cruises on the Mississippi, the Columbia and Snake Rivers in the Pacific Northwest, and the Hudson River in New York. They also have a fleet of small, coastal cruise ships that explore New England, Alaska, the Pacific Northwest, and the Southeast coast. Staterooms are large, and most include balconies. Other cabins offer a picture window that opens to the fresh outside air. Ports are visited every day, and tours focus on historic sites, homes, museums and other attractions of cultural interest. Ships reflect a modern take on early American décor, with an emphasis on comfort and informal luxury. The clientele is a somewhat older crowd, and children are uncommon. Daily cocktail hour and wine & beer with meals are included.

Why Choose American Cruise Lines?

American Cruise Lines is a fine choice for travelers interested in a river or small-ship coastal cruise that explores the diverse history, landscapes, cultures, architecture and cuisines of the United States. It is also ideal for US citizens looking for a relaxing and enriching vacation that keeps them close to home.

American Queen Steamboat Company

Founded	2011
Headquarters	Memphis, TN
Ownership	Private
Destinations	United States
Languages	English
Caters to	Older, well-traveled individuals with an interest in American history and culture
Known for	Traditional and frilly early American luxury décor, highly inclusive pricing
Dining	Multiple venues including an al fresco option
Evening Attire	Casual (no shorts)
Formal Nights	None
Slogan	*"Uniquely American River Cruises"*

Summary

American Queen Steamboat Company's fleet of cruise ships consists entirely of authentic paddle-wheeler riverboats, including its namesake *American Queen*, which is the largest river steamboat ever built. Ships range in size from 166 to 414 passengers, offer multiple dining venues, and feature a frilly early American décor with lots of lace, dark wood and antiques. Cruises focus on four river segments or combinations: Lower Mississippi, Upper Mississippi, Ohio-Tennessee-Cumberland, and Columbia & Snake. Fares include a pre-cruise hotel stay, wine & beer with dinner, meals in all dining venues, hotel-to-ship transfer, and shore excursions. Food is generally all-American and tailored to the particular locale.

Why Choose American Queen?

American history buffs, nostalgia aficionados, and pretty much anyone else who enjoys early American charm and old-school entertainment will have a great time on American Queen's paddle-wheeler ships. The small size of their vessels makes the voyage highly personalized and intimate.

Avalon Waterways

Founded	2004
Headquarters	Littleton, CO
Ownership	Globus Family of Brands
Destinations	Europe, China, Southeast Asia, South America, Galápagos Islands
Languages	English
Caters to	North America, UK and Australia
Known for	Cultural enrichment program, Suite Ships®, attentive service, free tours
Dining	Main dining room and two casual bistros with open seating
Evening Attire	Dressy Casual
Formal Nights	Captain's Dinner: Dressy Casual
Slogan	*"Unexpected. Unhindered. Utterly Unique River Cruises"*

Summary

Avalon Waterways brings a modern luxury motif to river cruising through their unique ships, each of which is designed to fit the uniqueness of the region it cruises. Staterooms on the newer suite-class vessels feature floor-to-ceiling retractable windows that give their French balcony more of a full-balcony effect. The line sails various rivers throughout Europe as well as the Mekong River in Vietnam and Cambodia, the Irrawaddy River in Myanmar (Burma), the Yangtze in China, and the Amazon River in Peru. For cruises to the Galápagos Islands, Avalon operates relatively small, intimate yachts that provide an up close and personal experience. Locally sourced beer & wine at meals, specialty coffees, WiFi, bicycles, and most shore excursions are included.

Why Choose Avalon Waterways?

For a more contemporary décor, yet still with the luxuries of a fine river cruise, Avalon Waterways fits the bill. Those interested in the Galápagos Islands will enjoy Avalon's intimate experience via their smaller yachts. Fares are reasonable, sailings have a unique personalization factor, and service is excellent.

Scenic Luxury Cruises & Tours

Founded	2008 (1986 as a tour operator)
Headquarters	Australia
Ownership	Australian (Private)
Destinations	Europe, Asia, Africa, Russia
Languages	English
Caters to	North America, UK, Australia
Known for	Relaxed and flexible culture, truly all-inclusive fares, group and GPS-guided independent tours, spacious ships ("Space Ships"), butlers for all cabins
Dining	Main dining room, specialty restaurant, casual café, Chef's Table (upper suites)
Evening Attire	Smart casual
Formal Nights	+/-2 dress-up gourmet dinners
Slogan	*"All-Inclusive Luxury"*

Summary

Australian-owned Scenic Luxury Cruises & Tours operates river cruise ships with more public space than most, facilitated by fewer passenger staterooms, thereby allowing unique features like a full fitness facility. The décor reflects a contemporary, hotel chic vibe with a focus on luxury and comfort. Suites are essentially larger versions of single-room staterooms with added seating, thereby sacrificing formality but providing more open space. The line's "Sun Lounge" balconies open to the outside via fully retractable windows and can be closed off from the cabin with folding glass doors. Service is key, and all staterooms come with a butler. The line also offers ocean cruises on its *Scenic Eclipse* "discovery yacht".

Why Choose Scenic?

Scenic is an appropriate choice for travelers seeking modern luxury, excellent service, flexibility, a relaxed atmosphere, and an authentic, all-inclusive experience that includes shore excursions, alcoholic beverages, gratuities, and use of the ship's electrically-assisted bicycles.

Tauck River Cruises

Founded	1925 (Tauck tour company)
Headquarters	Wilton, CT
Ownership	Tauck family (Private)
Destinations	Europe
Languages	English
Caters to	North America
Known for	Exclusive and highly unique shore excursions, all-inclusive pricing,
Dining	Main dining room and casual eatery with open seating, al fresco on sun deck
Evening Attire	Resort casual
Formal Nights	Special Occasion Evenings: Dressy
Slogan	*"How You See the World Matters"*

Summary

A branch of the long-established worldwide Tauck tour company, Tauck River Cruises offers sailings on major rivers in Europe. Ships are well-appointed, stylish and spacious with an onboard culture centered on relaxed sophistication. Most staterooms have floor-to-ceiling windows that open to French balconies. Tauck leverages off its worldwide tour company resources to provide unique and highly immersive shore excursions and enrichment lectures, with a few exclusives other lines can't offer. Three tour directors are assigned to each sailing. Fares are truly all-inclusive, with shore excursions, alcoholic beverages, gratuities, transfers, WiFi, and either a pre- or post-cruise hotel stay on the list.

Why Choose Tauck?

Tauck River Cruises is perfect for veteran travelers looking for a new and enriching vacation experience with access to exclusive tours and sites. Families spanning multiple generations may also find Tauck to be their best river cruise option, especially on sailings that have dedicated, family-oriented programs. Like most other river cruise lines, passengers can expect luxurious, comfortable surroundings along with gourmet food and extensive amenities.

Uniworld Boutique River Cruise Collection

Founded	1976
Headquarters	Los Angeles, CA
Ownership	The Travel Corporation
Destinations	Europe, China, Southeast Asia, Russia, Egypt, India
Languages	English
Caters to	Wealthy travelers in North America, the UK and Australia
Known for	Opulent luxury, all-inclusive fares, suite butlers, culinary excellence, antiques, original artwork, meticulous service
Dining	Varies by ship
Evening Attire	Smart casual
Formal Nights	Special events: jacket, cocktail dress
Slogan	*"You deserve the best"*

Summary

Clearly one of the most luxurious lines in river cruising, Uniworld offers cruises throughout Europe as well as China, Southeast Asia (Vietnam & Cambodia), Russia, Egypt and India. Ships are meticulous and sumptuously elegant, the interiors reminding one more of a Parisian palace than a cruise ship, with antiques and valuable pieces of original art throughout. Staterooms are comfortable and lushly decorated, with most offering marble bathrooms and a French balcony. Suites come with butler service. The highly inclusive fares in Europe cover all meals and beverages (including alcohol), gratuities, most shore excursions, airport transfers, WiFi, and the use of its bicycle fleet. The degree of alcoholic beverages inclusivity varies in other regions.

Why Choose Uniworld?

If you are an affluent, discerning traveler who enjoys opulence, highly attentive service and epicurean cuisine, Uniworld is ideal for you. Another draw is the opportunity to cruise rivers most other lines don't, like the Nile in Egypt and the Ganges River in India.

Viking River Cruises

Founded	1997
Headquarters	Los Angeles, CA
Ownership	Private
Destinations	Europe, Southeast Asia, China, Russia, Egypt
Languages	English
Caters to	North America, the UK and Australia
Known for	Scandinavian features, cultural enrichment, large staterooms, thoughtful service, fresh & healthy food
Dining	Main restaurant and two alternative venues, all with open seating
Evening Attire	Casual
Formal Nights	Captains Dinner: optional dress-up
Slogan	*"Exploring the World in Comfort"*

Summary

Viking is a powerhouse in the river cruise industry, and their huge fleet provides travelers with numerous voyage choices. Their signature Nordic-designed "Longships" are the largest river vessels in Europe, with less-common offerings like authentic outside balconies and two-room suites. Some Longships have a restaurant/lounge that can be converted to al fresco dining—a popular feature with passengers. Vessels have various voltage and plug configurations to suit each market, so check to see if you'll need an adapter or converter. Viking also sails the Yangtze River in China, the Mekong in Cambodia & Vietnam, the Irrawaddy in Myanmar (Burma), and the Nile in Egypt. Fares include all meals with complimentary wine & beer, shore excursions and WiFi.

Why Choose Viking?

Viking runs like a well-oiled machine with its attentive Swiss-trained staff and state-of-the-art ships. The line is a perfect choice for those who enjoy contemporary surroundings, an overall lack of pretense, fresh and healthy food choices, and lots of flexibility.

CHAPTER 16: BEST PRACTICES

Introduction

Cruises are somewhat different than other types of vacations, but an all-inclusive resort is probably the most comparable land-based example when it comes to guest interaction. Like a cruise, you have a large number of guests utilizing the same common areas and amenities over a number of days, though some will leave at times for excursions and return back to the resort. In one case, the resort remains stationary on land, while the other glides around the ocean to visit various ports of call.

Like air travel, there are both written and unwritten rules about dos and don'ts on a cruise, and I'm sure the vast majority of the people reading this book know what they are. Still, it helps to have a polite review, right?

To help, cruise ship crewmembers monitor any and all behavior that might affect the comfort, enjoyment, health, safety or well-being of the passengers and crew, and they take appropriate action as needed. This may even include discontinuing passage to those who cause excessive disruptions or risks.

So, let's look at some of the guidelines for any cruise vacation.

Don't Save Deck Lounges

It is frowned upon to place one's belongings on a lounge chair in the morning to "save" it, only to return hours later to bask in the sun. Fortunately, most cruise lines have adopted policies whereby crewmembers

monitor personal items and towels left on deck lounges and remove them if they remain unattended for more than 30 minutes. That allows plenty of time for someone to grab a slice of pizza and the tropical cocktail of the day without anyone disturbing their special spot. Arguments over lounge chairs are probably the most common altercations between passengers on a cruise.

Observe the Pool Rules

Cruise ship pools are exceptionally small relative to the number of people in and around them, which means the potential for injury and health issues are increased. Therefore, obeying the rules here is significantly more important than any public pool on land.

As I've mentioned before, cruise ship personnel are the best in the world at creating and maintaining a healthy environment, but they can't manage everything on their own. They need our help.

It's always a good idea to read the posted signs at the pool, but here are a few items that are often violated, as remarkable as they may seem.

Cruise ship pools are almost always shallow, so they are not suitable for diving or doing cannonballs. That's a great way to break an arm or a leg, not to mention causing a head or neck injury. These pools are better for wading, socializing, cooling off, harmlessly splashing around, and of course, the occasional volleyball tournament.

Running on a wet and slippery pool deck, which are often crowded, risks injuring multiple people at the same time. And what if someone's colorful tropical drink gets spilled? Egad!

Kids who are not potty-trained, including those in diapers (and even "swim diapers"), are not allowed in the pool because of obvious health concerns. For these little guys, I suggest sailing on a ship that has designated "splash zones" for kids, where they can frolic in the water to their heart's content.

Wash Your Hands

Cruise ships set the gold standard when it comes to cleanliness and preventing illness. In fact, you'll find one out of every ten crew members cleaning or disinfecting at any given time of day or night, from handrails and elevator buttons to touchscreens and fitness equipment. But it helps when passengers do their part.

This means thoroughly washing hands after using the facilities and taking advantage of motion-activated hand sanitizer stations throughout the ship. I recommend "taking a hit" of hand sanitizer at every station you pass, as it may save you from the person who brought a case of the flu on board and touched that handrail just before you did.

Don't Throw Food

Some people throw food off their stateroom balconies to watch seagulls swoop after it. Sure, it's entertaining, but there are better things to do with that piece of blueberry muffin that accidentally dropped to the floor, like depositing it in the trash bin.

The draft created by a moving ship almost always blows food or any other discarded debris back onto someone else's balcony, possibly while they're sitting out there enjoying a cup of coffee or tea. It's no fun stepping out on your veranda to find it littered with half-eaten food scraps.

Keep the Peace

One obvious, but often violated rule is to keep quiet on cabin decks during the late evening and early morning hours when people may be asleep. Keeping the noise down is just one of those common-sense practices to prevent negatively impacting other passengers' cruise experience.

Monitor the Kids

A big part of keeping the peace (above) is making sure children don't get out of hand. Sure, it's their vacation as much as anyone else's, and they have every right to have a great time, but running and screaming in the passageways late at night isn't respectful to other guests. After all, some people are late-night partyers, while others prefer to turn in after dinner and get up early to enjoy a quiet ship in the wee hours of the morning.

Cruises are particularly safe for kids, which is one reason why they are so popular for multi-generational vacations. It's not like a beach in Mexico where you might worry about a nefarious character scooping them up while you're not looking.

Consequently, parents tend to relax the rules a bit on cruises and allow the little ones some extra leeway. This is entirely appropriate, but perhaps it makes sense to tighten the reigns in the late evening hours.

Smoke in Designated Areas Only

Smoking is always prohibited in staterooms, including out on the balcony. It is also banned in most public spaces, although there's usually one or more designated outdoor areas where smoking is allowed. Larger ships may provide a cigar lounge with special ventilation, and a handful of cruise lines still allow smoking in portions of their casinos, but most companies are gradually banning it there as well.

The location on cruise ships where smoking violations occur most often is on the stateroom balcony. Since it's technically outside, people assume they won't bother other passengers or pose any risks, but that's not true. The draft of a moving cruise ship will blow smoke directly onto the next few downwind balconies, covering other passengers in secondhand smoke. Also, a piece of burning ash can easily travel through an open balcony door and land on the carpet or a bed, starting a fire. It's just not a good idea.

Don't Skip the Muster Drill

The mandatory Muster Drill, which takes place shortly before the ship sets sail on Embarkation Day, is a very important safety protocol required by maritime law and punishable by either a fine or refusal of passage or both. Still, that doesn't stop people from skipping it, particularly first-time cruisers who don't realize how important it is or who believe they won't get caught.

Au contraire, the muster station leader will take role and easily identify those who have skipped out. More often than not, this leads to taking a simple make-up drill, which I have personally never done, but I imagine it's similar to being sent to detention in high school. Still, there are those who have actually been fined and escorted off the ship by security, with no refunds or apologies.

That's too bad because the muster drill is kind of fun. Most people have already enjoyed a few cocktails, meaning they are relaxed and jovial, and it's a perfect time to make a few wisecracks to your fellow passengers while you wait for things to happen. When it's over, the sail away party atmosphere launches into action, and everyone is officially on vacation!

Don't Snub the Dress Code

Admittedly, cruise ship dress codes seem a little silly at times, if not vague, but the important thing is to get into the spirit of things. Dressing up may not be nearly as important today as it was in the Golden Era of cruising, but it's still a big deal to many of us, and it's a drag when people don't play along. Still, if someone shows up at a main dining room or gourmet specialty restaurant in the wrong attire, they'll usually be asked to kindly return to their stateroom and give it another try.

It feels celebratory and somewhat nostalgic to roam around the ship on dressier nights, seeing everyone in their fancy duds being elegant, fashionable, sexy, flashy, avant-garde, and everything in between. When you run across someone who clearly rejects the night's suggested attire...well, it takes away from the fun.

At least the evening dress codes have relaxed over the last decade or so, with cruise lines endeavoring to strike a compromise between stuffy, over-the-top formalwear and a sea of people in torn jeans and tank tops. The solution, for most, is to let people dress comfortably but tastefully most evenings, then add one or more dressy nights with loose guidelines that allow people to "show their stuff".

For lines like Oceania, which remain "country club casual" throughout the cruise without a designated dress-up night, passengers are still expected to adhere to certain standards, and some choose on their own to go dressier for dinner. A few lines still have outright formal nights, but most of those have relaxed their requirements to black-tie optional, allowing men to wear dark suits and ties instead of a tuxedo, if they prefer.

From my personal experience as a travel agent, men object to dressing up far more than women do, and I wish I had a dollar for every occasion a male client asked me, "do I really need to bring a sport coat? I'm going on vacation, for goodness sake!" But, at some point, their wife or girlfriend usually gets them back on track.

CHAPTER 17: TIPPING

KEVIN STREUFERT

Introduction

Tipping is a common conundrum among cruise passengers, especially when you consider that there's more to it than just who, when and how much to tip. It's also important to consider what gratuities you're  paying automatically and whether it makes sense to add a little more or let it be.

Cruise lines also differ in how they handle gratuities, particularly the luxury brands, so it's important to review the policies on your line's website. But for our purposes, we'll look at the most common practices on ocean cruise ships, and you can make adjustments if your situation is different.

Tipping the Crew

Most cruise lines charge passengers a daily service fee to cover gratuities for service members of the crew. This includes your cabin steward, his/her assistant (if any), servers in all the onboard restaurants including the main dining Room, and other behind-the-scenes service personnel. These people usually earn paltry base wages, meaning they count on our gratuities to make a decent living, so I encourage people not to feel as though they are being nickeled and dimed to death. The idea behind this compensation method, as opposed to charging higher cruise fares and paying greater base wages, is to promote better service by the staff.

The per-person charge varies by cruise line, but most use $13 to $16 per day, and slightly more if you're traveling in a suite. This "recommended" amount is typically added to your shipboard account unless you instruct Passenger Services/Guest Relations to increase, decrease, or eliminate it entirely. If you prefer, most lines will allow you to pay your gratuities in advance to avoid adding to that dreaded final bill!

If you received subpar service during your cruise and feel tempted to reduce or eliminate your daily charge, I encourage you to leave it as-is. This penalizes the entire crew, not just the individual from whom you received poor service. Instead, I suggest forgoing paying that person anything extra.

On the other hand, if a crewmember provided exceptional service to you or your family during the cruise, an additional tip (preferably in US Dollars) is advised. Sometimes, the cruise line will provide envelopes for these personal tips, but that's a rarity these days, and it's fine to just pass a little cash to these individuals on the last full day of the cruise. Do not wait until Disembarkation Day because you will have difficulties tracking people down. That may even include your cabin steward, who will be busy preparing staterooms for the next group of passengers.

So, the question is: who and how much should you tip? I'll give you some general guidelines, broken out by job title, but you'll still have to make some judgment calls based on the length of your cruise and how much time and effort the individual expended.

The first tippable staff you'll come across on your cruise vacation are the porters who take your checked luggage at the pier. I recommend tipping $1 to $2 per bag, but probably no less than $5 overall. If you forgot your luggage tags, and the porter has to prepare them for you, add a little more.

Your cabin steward is included in the daily gratuity charge, but if he or she is super-attentive and helpful, a little extra is appropriate. Depending on your level of accommodations, the length of the cruise, and the quality of service, this could be as little as $10 or as much as $50. If the steward has an assistant who pops up frequently with towels, flowers, ice and other helpful items, slip that person about half of what you're giving the steward.

If you have a suite with a butler, be prepared to tip him a bit more, as his list of duties is a bit longer than a cabin steward. In fact, butlers *expect* an extra tip at the end of the cruise, whereas others know they'll only receive something if they knock the ball out of the park. Still, his compensation should be commensurate with his level of service, starting at $10 per day, if not $15 or $20. For extraordinary service, some people may tip more, if not a great deal more. The category of your suite also plays a part, as an Owner's Suite butler will expect a larger tip than a Mini-Suite butler.

If you do have a butler, you either won't have a cabin steward, or his responsibilities will be diminished. Still, the butler will have an assistant of some sort, such as a cabin attendant with limited responsibilities like cleaning and replacing towels. You don't need to tip the assistant as much as you would a cabin steward, but if he earns an extra gratuity, go with roughly 50% of the cabin steward guidelines.

When it comes to bartenders and cocktail waitresses, keep in mind that bar tabs and drink packages usually include a 15% to 18% gratuity, so be careful not to double-tip. Most likely, there will be a blank on your ticket for gratuity, as if you haven't paid a tip yet, but it's usually meant for a supplemental amount. But, that extra gratuity on your ticket is typically added to the "ship-wide pot", and it will be shared with the rest of the wait staff all over the vessel. If you want *your* favorite person to receive a little extra, track him/her down toward the end of the cruise and slip them some cash. Depending on how well and how often they helped you, I suggest anywhere from $10 to $20.

If you have an unlimited drink package, you may receive a zero-dollar ticket for every drink your order, which you are obligated to sign. Like a regular ticket, there should be a blank for a tip. But, since the price of your package included gratuities, you shouldn't feel obligated to add anything. Again, if someone has been particularly helpful, slip them a little cash later.

Restaurant wait staff are also compensated through the daily gratuity charge. In fact, the program is particularly beneficial to them since anytime dining and specialty restaurants have all but eliminated having the same table and wait staff at dinner throughout one's cruise. Without that repetition, waiters can't establish a rapport with passengers and earn a cash gratuity, so the daily gratuity charge ensures they get paid. That means they don't expect anything extra, but if you're in an unusual situation where one or two waiters took exceptional care of you throughout a cruise, feel free to slip them an extra $10 or $20 on the last night.

In the old days, it was customary to tip your maître d' at the Main Dining Room, but they are now part of the professional staff and do not normally expect tips. However, if he performs a special service such as arranging for a birthday cake to be brought to the table, it's customary to slip him $5 or $10.

Room service on most ships is free, but it's a nice gesture to slip your room service waiter a few dollars when he arrives with your food, even though he may be covered under the auto-gratuity program. The amount should be loosely based on how much you've ordered. But, if you can't get to your wallet or don't have any small bills, don't sweat it. Room service waiters only receive tips part of the time and consider it an extra treat when it happens.

Just as you would expect to do on land, spa therapists and salon technicians at sea expect a gratuity for their services. But, on a cruise ship, you should expect 15% to 18% to be automatically added to your bill. That means you should exercise the same caution as you would with a bar tab by not routinely tipping a full amount. Decide whether the service you received was worth more than the default gratuity, and only add extra if that was the case. For example, if your massage therapist gives you a hard sell on spa products after your treatment, which sometimes happens, perhaps it makes sense to put a zero in that box.

An alternative strategy that has worked well for many veteran cruisers is to provide a tip at the *beginning* of the cruise to those who will be providing services throughout the voyage, thereby setting the stage for exceptional service. This is often accompanied by a promise for an additional tip at the end. I personally haven't done this, but it should work well for cabin stewards, butlers, and your favorite bartender at the lounge or bar where you plan to spend a lot of time.

> **TIP:** Before you leave for your trip, make sure you have a wide assortment of ones, fives, tens and twenties for tipping purposes. Keep this money separate from your spending money to ensure you always have it available.

Tipping Tour Guides & Drivers

Most likely, you will participate in one or more shore excursions during your cruise, which will be booked through the cruise line or a reputable third-party like Shore Trips. However, the operator will be a local tour company with employees who count on tips for their livelihood.

Given the various people and transportation options that may be involved with shore excursions, tipping can be a challenge, but let's establish a few guidelines to work from.

If you go on a simple excursion that involves only a tour guide and a bus driver, plan on tipping the tour guide as you leave the bus and say goodbye. If it's a large bus full of people, $5 or the equivalent in local currency is perfectly adequate. If you're in a small group, $20 or more may be more appropriate. Just try to gauge what that tour guide would have made with a larger group and increase your share accordingly.

It's also important to be sure the driver is covered (unless the tour guide and driver are one and the same). Tip him/her a few dollars separately if it isn't made clear that tips will be shared. In some cases, the driver will place a jar or cup at the front of the bus for his or her personal tips.

In cases where you board a boat operated by a multi-person crew, there should be a tip jar somewhere on board. Otherwise, you'll hand your tip to a crewmember at the end as you step off the vessel, and you can count on all the tips being shared with the rest of the crew. Again, if you're in a large group of people, $5 should be fine, but you might go to $10 for a longer and particularly enjoyable tour.

If you're part of a small group, such as a half dozen or fewer people on a fishing expedition, it makes sense to tip $20 or more.

314

Even further, if you are a private party of two, $40 or $50 ($80 to $100 in total) is more appropriate.

Tipping gets even more complicated when you are transported to your tour boat on a motorcoach that has both a tour guide and a driver. Indeed, it is customary to tip everyone involved, but feel free to reduce the amounts accordingly. For example, if you are a couple traveling together, you might slip the bus tour guide $5 for both of you instead of individually.

CHAPTER 18: SNAGS & SOLUTIONS

Seasickness

For most of us, there's a unique magic in traversing the ocean on a grand ship as we watch the water stream by with a glass of wine in-hand. Then there's the gentle roll of the vessel, echoing the sensation of being rocked to sleep like a baby. Yet, for an unfortunate few who are hyper-sensitive to motion, the experience may not be so fun.

If you've experienced queasiness on a deep-sea fishing trip or catamaran coastal cruise because of the boat's constant bobbing and rocking from the waves, rest assured that the motion of a cruise ship is entirely different. Small boats bop over waves with quick and sudden movements, while cruise ships cut through them and react slowly. In other words, rough seas have a completely different and far less dramatic effect. If you or a loved one is still concerned about contracting *mal de mer*, there are steps you can take to lessen the risk.

First, select the newest and largest ship available for your destination of choice. Newer ships will feature the latest in stabilization technology, and larger vessels are less susceptible to ocean turbulence than smaller ones. For example, the Oasis-Class ships offered by Royal Caribbean weigh 225,000 gross tons and have the water displacement of a Nimitz-class aircraft carrier, so it should come as no surprise that they handle rough seas better than midsize cruise ships in the 80,000-ton range.

Second, select a cabin in the center of the ship on a lower deck even though the swankier choices are usually higher up. The most common movement cruise passengers feel is the "roll" or port-to-starboard sway of the ship, so you'll want a location with the least effect. Think of the vertical axis of the ship like a pendulum, where the side-to-side distance of travel is the least at the bottom and most at the top. That's exactly how it will feel on board if seas are rough. A similar phenomenon holds true at the center of the horizontal access (middle of the ship), where the pitch from bow to stern is less noticeable.

Third, upgrade to a balcony stateroom if your budget allows it, as you'll have a sliding glass door to let in restorative fresh air. If you're feeling queasy, you can step outside and gaze (don't do a fixed stare) at the horizon, thereby tricking your brain into thinking you're still.

If conditions are normal, and you're on a larger cruise ship, you'll hardly notice any motion at all. In fact, oceangoing enthusiasts sometimes complain about the absence of movement on newer megaships, as they prefer the traditional feel of being on the water.

Fourth, consider taking a "test run" on an Alaska Inside Passage cruise to see how you do. Very little of that trip will take place on the open seas, especially if you sail round trip out of Vancouver, and the experience will go a long way toward helping you graduate to the next level. Besides, removing all the unknowns about cruise travel itself will make future voyages all that more enjoyable, regardless of the conditions.

Finally, bring one or more motion-sickness medicines on the trip, just in case. If your sensitivity to motion is historically severe, consider using them as a preventative measure instead of a treatment, as they are usually more effective that way. Be sure to consult with your doctor to find out whether an over-the-counter medicine like Dramamine or a prescription drug is better for you. There are also some excellent homeopathic remedies out there.

Seasickness is also partially psychodynamic, so it helps to keep the mind occupied. It's also a good idea to spend plenty of time out on deck in the fresh air, even if you've sprung for that balcony stateroom. Mix things up, and absorb the reality that you're on the equivalent of a small city, safe and sound. It's also smart to keep your stomach relatively full. Try to eat normally, and don't skip meals because you're feeling queasy. An empty stomach only adds to the condition.

If you're taking a longer cruise, rest assured that virtually everyone gets their "sea legs", no matter how motion-sensitive they are. The brain ultimately adjusts, and most people feel the slightest wave sensation for a day or two after the cruise, as the body's self-imposed counterbalance takes time to burn off.

Of course, no one can control the weather, so there's always a slight chance of negotiating through a heavy storm with turbulent seas. Cruise lines will try their best to alter itineraries or routes to avoid them, but that's not always possible. Just keep in mind that these situations aren't common.

> **TIP:** Several of my clients have reported prescription Scopolamine patches to be effective for seasickness. There are also holistic treatments such as ginger candy, cookies and pills. Green apples are another popular remedy, and room service is always ready to bring them to your cabin.

Illness and Injuries

Injuries or falling ill can happen to anyone, anywhere, at any time. We are all prepared for such eventualities at home, but it becomes a challenge while traveling abroad, including on a cruise ship.

That being said, would you be surprised to hear that cruise ships are among the healthiest places on Earth? The press does a great job of making us think otherwise. But if we managed our own environment and daily routine like a cruise ship, we'd avoid getting sick and be much healthier.

Cruise ship personnel are experts at keeping germs at bay and healing sick passengers quickly. They have a financial incentive to do so because the negative press from a "sick ship" affects bookings, and passengers sequestered to their cabins with the flu aren't roaming the ship spending money. As a result, cruises have established the gold standard for avoiding the flu, colds and digestive diseases.

If you've ever ventured out early or stayed up late on a cruise ship, you've probably noticed the hive of cleaning personnel disinfecting every possible high-touch surface from handrails and elevator buttons to computer keyboards and gym equipment.

These people fade into the background as the ship's common areas get busier, but approximately 1 staff member for each 10 passengers on board is always cleaning. That's because fingers and hands carry countless germs and do a great job of distributing them around.

Research suggests that during the next hour, you'll touch your mouth eight times, your nose five times, and your eyes three times. And, who knows what germy surfaces you might have touched in between. We are, by nature, very effective creatures at spreading disease.

That's why cruise personnel are so diligent about cleaning, and it's the reason they place hand sanitizer stations all over the ship. I encourage everyone to "take a hit" whenever they pass by one of those stations because you honestly don't know who might have stepped on board with a fledgling case of the flu, feeling no symptoms until a day or two later after spreading it around. And, if you touch a handrail shortly after they do…

But what about the Norovirus, also known as the "Cruise Ship Disease"?

According to the CDC, 99% of Norovirus cases are contracted on land, not on cruise ships. Don't buy into this myth, which has been dramatized by the press. The truth is, you are exponentially more likely to contract the Norovirus in a hotel where common surfaces are disinfected far less diligently.

I'll stick with the cruise ship, thank you very much.

Should you actually fall ill or injure yourself while on a cruise ship, the onboard medical center is just a few decks away, and the medical staff is capable of dealing with virtually any non-life-threatening issue. But even in emergency situations, shipboard facilities are usually adequate to keep a patient stable until they can be transported to the nearest critical-care facility.

That being said, there's one thing you should keep in mind if you're feeling under the weather and head to the ship's doctor. If he or she suspects you may be afflicted with a flu or virus that could potentially be transmitted to the crew or other passengers, you may be quarantined to your stateroom for a good portion of your cruise as a precaution. Keep that in mind if it feels like you have just a minor cold or allergies.

Quarantining sick passengers is a smart and effective practice that prevents those rare outbreaks on cruise ships that are always publicized on the news. Therefore, I'm in full support of it and would never encourage anyone to roam around a cruise ship with flulike symptoms. I'm simply suggesting a little prudent self-evaluation before making a beeline for the ship's doctor "just in case".

Also, shipboard medical centers can get expensive, and standard health insurance usually doesn't cover the cost. At best, it will be treated as an out-of-network expense and may be counted toward your annual deductible.

I recommend checking on the details of your personal health coverage before leaving on any trip. If it falls short, you have another reason to consider buying travel protection. See the **Travel Insurance** section at the end of this chapter.

Course/Itinerary Changes

Cruise ship captains don't change their scheduled itineraries at the drop of a hat, but when events occur outside of their control, a course or destination change may be inevitable. Anything that has the potential of threatening the ship, its passengers or the crew will be evaluated. This includes severe weather, rough seas, civil unrest at or near the next port of call, or even a technical issue rendering the port unable to accommodate your ship on the scheduled day.

In most cases, the captain and crew will make other arrangements, such as a substitute port of call—hopefully one that offers a similar experience to the port being dropped. Of course, this causes a frenzy as passengers rush to book tours for the new port while shore excursion personnel scramble to determine what they can offer. This will depend on which cruise line-sanctioned tour operators are available for the impromptu arrival and how much capacity has been absorbed by other cruise ships already scheduled to be at the new port that day.

Fortunately, everyone can rest assured that any tours booked through the cruise line or a reputable company like *Shore Trips* will be refunded in full if the ship doesn't successfully arrive at a scheduled port. Just be sure to request that refund, as it may not come automatically.

In the event a course change is implemented to navigate around severe weather, the ship may still be able to reach the next port of call, possibly even on time, as cruise schedules are typically based on ships traveling at less than full speed.

It it's a few hours late, another shore excursion frenzy will erupt around whether booked tours have enough time to run. Sometimes everything, including the ship's departure time, can be pushed back a couple of hours to allow tours to operate as planned, but that's not always possible. The only sure thing is a logistical nightmare for shore excursion personnel, and it's important for passengers to find patience during that process.

No one, including cruise ship captains, can predict the weather 100% of the time. That means cruise vessels will occasionally be burdened with navigating through unexpected rough seas. By the time that becomes a reality, a course change may no longer be an option.

In the event of a significant disruption to a cruise, even those resulting from an act of nature, the cruise line will usually make an effort to compensate passengers for their inconvenience or distress, the extent of which will be proportional to the severity of the situation. This could be a small voucher to be applied toward a future sailing or, with an unusually difficult case, a free future cruise or a complete refund. Such occurrences are rare, and the cruise line has a lot of leeway in deciding the type and amount of compensation to offer.

Passenger Cancellations

When it comes to cruises, there are two types of cancellations:

- Those initiated by the passenger to cancel their trip
- Those initiated by the cruise line to cancel the cruise

Passengers who cancel their own vacation are subject to the cruise line's cancellation policies. Every line has its own penalty schedule, which can be modified at any time, though any such changes will be applicable to new bookings only. If you booked a special promotion, it may have its own cancellation policy, especially if it entails a reduced deposit. Therefore, I always recommend finding out the specific cancellation policy for your potential booking in advance.

Still, a "normal" booking without a reduced up-front deposit usually allows for a full refund until the final payment date for the cruise—usually 90 days in advance. Once the cruise is paid in full, the penalty for cancelling grows higher and higher as the sail date approaches, eventually becoming 100% non-refundable roughly a week or so prior to sailing, sometimes earlier.

Most people avoid the risk of losing the rather large up-front investment in a cruise vacation by purchasing travel insurance (aka "travel protection") when they make their final payment. The cost of this insurance is often less than the taxes for the cruise, so many passengers feel the expenditure is worthwhile.

There are many factors to consider before buying travel protection, so be sure to read the section on **Travel Insurance** at the end of this chapter.

Cruise Line Cancellations

Let's face it. Life is a highly fluid situation where the unexpected spontaneously happens. In the cruise industry, you never know when a ship will experience a rare mechanical issue, a kitchen fire, or some other mishap that sends it to the nearest shipyard for repairs. Most issues can be

fixed in a matter of days, but it will inevitably result in the cancellation of the cruises on which those days encroach.

It's also possible for severe weather, particularly hurricanes, to trigger the cancellation of a cruise. Essentially, if the cruise line deems *any* condition to pose undue risk to its passengers or crew, it will forgo the revenue and cancel the sailing. That's the responsible thing to do, after all.

The problem with cruise line cancellations, on the rare occasions when they happen, is that they almost always occur at the last minute, thereby making it difficult for passengers to make alternate vacation plans. These days, it seems like all worthwhile travel options fill up far in advance. That means if the next best thing isn't already full, it will probably come at a high price.

Cruise lines have some discretion as to how they compensate you for a cancellation. But, at the very least, you can expect a full refund of your cruise fare and any other advance expenditures you made with the cruise line. Most likely, they will add a voucher for future travel. If you have purchased non-refundable airline tickets, a refund of the non-refundable amount (usually the rebooking fee) may be offered.

It's also possible to be bumped off your cruise if someone arranges to charter the entire ship during your sailing. But this usually happens far in advance, giving you plenty of time to make alternate vacation arrangements, and you can expect similar compensation to what's described above.

Missing Your Ship

I have never had a client miss their cruise ship, and I doubt I ever will. That's because I make sure they have plenty of extra time in case there's an air travel delay or other mishap that might otherwise prevent them from getting to the port on time. Usually, I schedule them to fly into the embarkation city at least one day in advance, especially if the departure port is outside the US. On rare occasion, if a client is traveling from one major US city to another

327

on a super-early flight, and there are numerous later flights that would still get them to the port on time, I might make an exception. But, if the trip is scheduled during wintertime, and one airport or the other is historically prone to winter-weather closures or delays, I'll insist they fly over the day before.

Nevertheless, people do miss their cruise ships from time to time, most often because of flight delays, and the only option is to catch up with that vessel at its next port of call. If the delay is outside of your control, and you purchased a quality travel insurance policy through your travel agent or cruise line, the costs to fly you to the next port should be covered.

Alternatively, if you have a premium credit card with a hefty annual fee, it may offer travel protection as a cardholder benefit. If you used that card to pay for your trip, they might pay for your travel disruption costs and put you back on track with your cruise ship ASAP. I always advise my clients to be aware of the exact travel protection available to them before leaving on any trip and make sure it fits their personal risk tolerance.

Whether you're using an insurance policy or credit cardholder benefit, you will have an emergency number to call once missing your ship becomes inevitable. If you're dealing with a quality organization, this will put you in contact with a concierge who will handle your alternate travel arrangements.

If you don't have travel protection, getting to the next port and the related costs including airfare, hotels and transfers, will be at your expense. In such a case, your first call should be to your travel agent, who has better resources to resolve the situation than you do. If you didn't book your trip through a travel agent, call the customer service department of the cruise line, and they can help walk you through the process.

If you are late returning to your ship at a port of call, you may or may not miss your ship. Cruise ship captains frequently wait for late passengers, but it depends on a number of factors, not the least of which is how late you actually are. It also depends on how many other people are tardy, meaning the larger your rag-tag group of delinquents, the better off you'll be!

The port's regulations and docking schedule are also a factor. If, for example, there's another vessel waiting for your ship's berth, the captain may have no choice but to hightail it out of there. Otherwise, it is entirely at his or her discretion how long the ship will remain at the pier beyond its scheduled departure.

Should you be on a shore excursion that was sold to you by the cruise line, your chances get slightly better, but the ship can only wait so long. If necessary, it will leave you behind. Just take comfort in knowing that the cruise line and any reputable third-party tour provider will guaranty your return to the ship and cover all costs of getting you back on board, even if it means flying you to the next port of call.

If you plan to do your own thing in port, be sure you have the correct time, which can change unexpectedly from one port to the next. You will find a notice of such changes in your daily program. There is also a slight chance the ship's time and local time will be different, so be sure to confirm which time zone the "all aboard" deadline is based on. Finally, it's always a good idea to plan your return to the ship at least an hour early, thereby providing an allowance for any unexpected delays.

TIP: If you are returning from a shore excursion, and your bus is caught in gridlock traffic—a common occurrence in places like St. Petersburg, Russia—keep in mind that many of your fellow passengers are "in the same boat". In cases like this, the ship will often wait for hours until every passenger is back on board, so try not to stress out.

Lost or Delayed Luggage

It is highly unlikely that your luggage will be lost or significantly delayed when it is in the hands of your cruise-ship porters. Managing baggage on and off a passenger ship may be a mammoth task, but it isn't all that complicated or fraught with potential errors.

Luggage typically goes missing in conjunction with air travel, although theft is also possible. In fact, one of my clients and her family had their luggage stolen from their rental car while eating lunch at a land-based restaurant. Fortunately, this occurred *after* their cruise, and their Allianz travel policy covered the replacement of their belongings.

Once you've confirmed that a piece of luggage has gone missing, your first order of business is to report the incident to the party who was responsible for it. In most cases, this will be the airline, and you'll need to file a baggage loss report at their customer service desk, usually next to baggage claim.

If the airline successfully delivers the bag to you a few hours later, and it causes little or no disruption to your trip, consider the case closed. But if the situation becomes a hardship, especially when it becomes evident that days may pass before your luggage catches up with you, it's time to report the incident to your travel insurance provider or credit card company (if your cardholder benefits include travel coverage).

Most likely, you will receive an allowance for the costs of your disruption, specifically to buy clothes, toiletries and cosmetics to bridge the gap until your luggage arrives. If your suitcase is ultimately designated as being lost, you will receive compensation for the cost of the bag and all its contents. However, determining the value of those items can be tricky, and you will probably be asked to make a detailed list including estimated replacement values.

If you don't have travel insurance, the airline may still reimburse you for your lost possessions. Likewise, if your luggage is simply delayed, they may cover the cost of a few replacement items up to a limit. They will usually require the original receipts of such purchases before reimbursing you, so be sure to keep them.

TIP: If you are ever a victim of theft while traveling and hope to recoup the loss through any insurance, it's helpful to have the local police file a report of the incident.

Travel Insurance

Travel insurance may seem like another clever way for airlines, cruise ship companies and other travel providers to nickel and dime us to death, much like the pricey checked luggage fees on your flight to the departure

port. But statistics prove that travel insurance is a prudent thing to buy, and Federal law requires travel providers and travel agents to offer it in conjunction with any booking. In the event a traveler declines such coverage, the law requires proof of such refusal via an online check box, voice recording, signed waiver, email, or other written media.

Travel insurance for cruises covers a number of items. First and foremost, it reimburses most (if not all) of a person's non-refundable cruise fare if they are forced to cancel their trip for a covered reason such as an illness, death in the family, loss of employment, jury duty, military deployment, and other items outside the traveler's control. Insurance purchased from your cruise line often comes in the form of a voucher for future travel, which may or may not be acceptable to you. If you would prefer a cash refund, there are third-party options with reputable insurance companies you may wish to consider. Ask your travel agent for guidance on this.

Travel policies also typically reimburse medical expenses, up to a limit, that are not covered by the individual's health insurance plan. In addition, there are allowances for lost or delayed luggage, trip delays, trip interruptions, and other items.

However, a line item that habitually falls short with standard cruise line protection is medical evacuation, which can cost upwards of $500,000 should someone need to be airlifted off a ship in the middle of the ocean. Most standard cruise line policies (and credit cardholder benefits) only cover $25,000 to $50,000 for this expense. So, be sure the policy you choose is adequate, or find comfort in the low probability of such an occurrence. It all depends on your level of health and personal risk tolerance.

Travel policies can be purchased directly from the cruise line or through your travel agent, who may be able to offer better coverage at similar pricing from a large insurance company like Allianz, CSA, HTH or John Hancock. For a higher premium, one can usually purchase a policy that allows the traveler to cancel their trip for any reason whatsoever.

Finally, if you have a super-premium credit card and use it to charge your cruise fare, check to see if your cardholder benefits include travel protection. The coverage is typically not as extensive as a full-fledged travel policy and probably doesn't include medical expenses, but you might find it acceptable for your trip, thereby negating the need to purchase additional insurance. The key is to pull together all the details and make an informed decision that suits your personal needs and risk tolerance.

CHAPTER 19: CRUISE LINE PERKS AND PROMISES

Loyalty Programs

Like all travel loyalty programs, cruise line versions reward frequent guests for their regular business and entice members to sail again with exclusive offers and incentives. If you are heading out on a first cruise, the primary passenger will automatically become a member of the cruise line's program upon their return, most likely at the entry-level tier (unless, say, you take a 21-day cruise in a suite, in which case you'll probably qualify for a higher loyalty level).

Depending on the cruise line, other passengers in the stateroom may or may not be automatically enrolled in the program, so if there's any chance they'll cruise again with that line, make sure to register them. This can usually be done online after the first cruise, and sometimes even before the cruise. If the latter is possible, membership will show up in "preview" status until the first cruise is completed.

The difference between cruise line programs and airline or hotel programs is that points aren't accumulated for the purpose of redemption. Instead, members accrue points or cruise nights for the purpose of reaching higher membership tiers, each of which offers more generous benefits on future cruises. Suite guests usually earn double points during each sailing.

Introductory-level members usually have access to special discounted rates on future sailings, many of which will be last-minute offers. They may also enjoy priority check-in at the pier and special onboard offers during their next cruise.

Higher levels gradually include benefits like priority embarkation/debarkation, discounts on suites and balconies, free stateroom upgrades, welcome stateroom amenities like wine and flowers, a private departure lounge, a private venue for breakfast on board, member cocktail parties, a dinner with the ship's officers, premium seating at theater events, and priority wait-listing for shore excursions, spa services and dining reservations.

For those reaching tier levels in the hundreds of nights (or points), a free cruise is often awarded.

Cruise Industry Passenger Bill of Rights

All Members of the Cruise Lines International Association ("CLIA") are dedicated to the comfort and care of all passengers on oceangoing cruises throughout the world. To fulfill this commitment, CLIA Members have agreed to adopt the following set of passenger rights:

1. The right to disembark a docked ship if essential provisions such as food, water, restroom facilities and access to medical care cannot adequately be provided on board, subject only to the Master's concern for passenger safety and security and customs and immigration requirements of the port.
2. The right to a full refund for a trip that is canceled due to mechanical failures, or a partial refund for voyages that are terminated early due to those failures.
3. The right to have available on board ships operating beyond rivers or coastal waters full-time, professional emergency medical attention, as needed until shore side medical care becomes available.
4. The right to timely information updates as to any adjustments in the itinerary of the ship in the event of a mechanical failure or emergency, as well as timely updates of the status of efforts to address mechanical failures.
5. The right to a ship crew that is properly trained in emergency and evacuation procedures.
6. The right to an emergency power source in the case of a main generator failure.
7. The right to transportation to the ship's scheduled port of disembarkation or the passenger's home city in the event a cruise is terminated early due to mechanical failures.
8. The right to lodging if disembarkation and an overnight stay in an unscheduled port are required when a cruise is terminated early due to mechanical failures.

9. The right to have included on each cruise line's website a toll-free phone line that can be used for questions or information concerning any aspect of shipboard operations.
10. The right to have this Cruise Industry Passenger Bill of Rights published on each line's website.

ABOUT THE AUTHOR

Kevin Streufert is a Cruise Planners® travel agency franchise owner, a full-time travel advisor, and a long-established writer of fiction and non-fiction books and articles.

His fiction works have been published under multiple pen names, but he is best known for the *Jack Lazar Series* of action thrillers, which he writes as **Kevin Sterling**. Each novel takes place in a different country to which he has traveled, and several have become Amazon #1 Best Sellers.

Other credits include co-authoring the MBA's *Handbook of Commercial Real Estate Finance* and publishing numerous articles in trade magazines, newspapers and online blogs about travel, commercial real estate, structured finance, creative writing and relationships.

Kevin holds a Master Cruise Counselor (MCC) designation, granted by the Cruise Lines International Association (CLIA) after an extensive program of classroom and online training, exams, case studies, cruise experience, ship inspections, significant client bookings, and attendance at industry events. He is ever-immersed in continuing education and stays at the forefront of cruise industry developments every day.

Kevin has traveled extensively throughout his life, starting with many summers in Europe growing up. Since then, he has diligently explored the world, including dozens of cruises and over 4 million miles in the air.

It's safe to say that travel and cruising are in his blood.

Kevin and his wife Deborah live in Denver, Colorado with their Golden Retriever, Shelby.

CPSIA information can be obtained
at www.ICGtesting.com
Printed in the USA
BVHW050449201218
536071BV00015B/2045/P

9 781540 352606